THE GRADUATE'S ALMANAC

The Definitive Guide for Life After School

www.CapandCompass.com

LEGAL INFORMATION

ISBN-13: 978-0-578-75651-6

The authors and Cap & Compass, Inc. have made their best efforts to be accurate and complete when preparing this book. The content of the book is not guaranteed to produce any particular result and is for general informational purposes only. In addition, the advice and explanations given in the book may not fit every individual's circumstances.

Therefore, the authors and Cap & Compass, Inc. do not assume responsibility for advice or information given. As a result, each reader should consider his or her specific circumstances when making decisions related to any of the topics covered in this book.

The authors and Cap & Compass, Inc. are not in the business of rendering legal, financial, or any other professional advice. Should questions regarding legal, financial, or professional advice arise, the reader should seek professional assistance.

The authors and Cap & Compass, Inc. shall not be held liable for any damages or losses caused by errors, inaccuracies, or omissions arising from direct or indirect use of this book.

This book was updated in 2021. Purchase single copies at Amazon.com or bulk orders at CapandCompass.com.

CONTENTS

CONTENTS

INTRODUCTION

When you're in school, you learn how to draw demand curves, write about American politics, and diagram carbon atoms. Although these topics are important, they're not very helpful when you need to find an apartment, pick health insurance, or fill out your taxes. Who explains life after school?

Cap & Compass has created *The Graduate's Almanac*, a follow-up to our previous book, *life after school. explained.* You can read from cover to cover or turn to the appropriate topic as you reach your first day on the job, business dinner, tax season, or any other milestone.

This book was written with recent graduates in mind, but the topics are useful for anyone who eats, spends money, pays taxes, or works for a living.

We do not intend for this book to be a substitute for the advice of professional accountants, financial advisors, apartment brokers, and so on. Rather, it is designed to help you get a basic understanding of the concepts and lingo. This foundation will help you to have meaningful conversations with professionals in order to make the best decisions for you. So next time your HR manager wants to talk to you about your 401(k) or HMO, you'll have the secret decoder.

Throughout the book, you will see Alex, a new graduate. Alex is a fictional character, the subject of all of our anecdotes, and a front for all of our embarrassing stories. This book was compiled from the experiences of many recent graduates—our friends, our co-workers, our previous readers—plus professionals from many fields.

If you have feedback or ideas that would make this book better, we would love to hear from you. Please send us an email at feedback@capandcompass.com.

We hope you enjoy!

"That the powerful play goes on, and you may contribute a verse. What will your verse be?"

– John Keating

(Stream Dead Poets Society. *You'll thank us later.)*

SECTION ONE:

WORK

Dracula's business dinner took a turn for the worse.

BUSINESS DINNERS

OVERVIEW

Odd food, small talk, and three different forks are the recipe for looking unprofessional. If you want to look smart at your job, then this topic is for you.

Everyone knows a little bit about fancy dinners from countless movies where the characters create chaos while engaging in witty banter and uproarious food fights.

Now we're going to take your working knowledge one step further. Since most people know what *not* to do at dinner, we'll tackle the stuff that you *should* do.

We'll cover etiquette and all the other things you'll need to know for a fancy meal. You'll get the inside skinny on social graces, learn fancy words like foie gras, and understand the dos and don'ts for different dishes, like sushi and steak.

We'll focus most of this chapter on the business dinner, but the advice applies to any number of situations. Many job interviews, family gatherings, and first dates take place over a nice dinner.

Read on!

THE THREE GOLDEN RULES

1. NOT THERE TO EAT

Now, down to the business of decoding the business dinner.

Eating might be your number-one priority, but it's not the number-one priority of your boss. This is not a pie-eating contest.

A WORK DINNER IS A SOCIAL OCCASION WITH AN AGENDA.

A dinner may start a lasting relationship with a client or close an important business deal.

Relax, and remember the goals of the dinner while at the table.

2. BE DISCREET

If you're just out of school, you're invited to be part of the evening, not the star.

When we talk to human resources staff about new hires, they are always quick to mention:

"NEW HIRES TRY TOO HARD TO IMPRESS THEIR COLLEAGUES."

Don't try to be an expert on company issues. Show that you are interested and informed, but don't call attention to yourself.

Everyone knows that you're relatively young and inexperienced. But don't remind them of this fact.

3. FOLLOW YOUR HOST

Your host is the person who decides to have the meal, invites the guests, and is usually called "boss" around the office.

Since you're not paying,

YOU NEED TO FOLLOW THE LEAD SET BY YOUR HOST.

If you follow along well, you won't stand out from the crowd. (In this situation, that's good.)

Think of the dinner experience as one of those games you played in elementary school, like Simon Says or Follow the Leader. (Weren't those the days?) Simon is the host, and you follow Simon's lead. We'll refer to the host as Simon over the course of this topic.

If Simon orders dessert, you can order dessert. If Simon wants to jump out of a plane, strap on your parachute. If Simon wants to hang out and chat about country pop, you make sure that you can't say enough about early Taylor Swift.

SIDEBAR

"Early Taylor Swift" would loosely be defined as the period between 2006 and 2013.

Items worthy of discussion would include Taylor's early hits, such as "Teardrops on My Guitar" and "Our Song," followed by a string of hits like "Love Song" and "You Belong With Me," to name a few.

Additionally, marvel at how Taylor's *Fearless* bagged Grammy Awards for both Best Country Album and, more impressively, Album of the Year in 2010—making her the youngest winner of the top honor to that point.

SEATING

MAITRE D'

Most dinners start the same way. Someone escorts you to your table. Often, this person is called a maitre d'. The maitre d' is your welcoming presence at the restaurant.

The "D" may pull your chair out for you to help you get seated or put your napkin on your lap. He or she is not flirting. Just say thank you and move on.

If you have any problems over the course of your meal, the "D" will help you out. Do not call him or her "the 'D'" in front of your host. As you've already guessed, this won't make you look professional.

NAPKINS

If the maitre d' doesn't take care of your napkin, seize the moment and do so yourself.

Placing your napkin on your lap seems like such a simple thing to remember, but it's so easy to forget. After 15 minutes, you'll realize that everyone else has a napkin on his or her lap, and you still have an origami swan staring at you.

Keep your napkin on your lap at all times. If you need to excuse yourself at any point, put your napkin in your chair, not back on the table. A napkin on the table may be seen by your server as a signal that you're finished with your meal, and your plate may be taken.

IGNORE THE MENU

Once you are seated, do not pick up the menu. Remember: this is not a pie-eating contest.

Talk to those around you. Create a comfortable atmosphere. You will be fed, we promise.

Keep an eye on Simon. Once Simon picks up his or her menu, you can start to look at your choices.

SMALL TALK

You may not know many of the people at your table. To avoid an uncomfortable silence, prior to the meal, ask about the people joining you to find out a little about them. Don't stalk them, but find out what they do or if they work with someone you know.

You also might want to freshen up on current events, sports, or other potential common interests. Unless Simon starts it, steer clear of inflammatory issues. And if Simon starts it, don't make it your mission to finish it.

HANDSHAKE

Once you introduce yourself, it's always nice to extend your hand. The proper handshake involves eye contact and a firm, three-second grip. That's it. Anything else is hand jive and could be seen as too much.

Unfortunately, many people's handshakes can be classified into one of two categories:

The Fish: a limp shake with no eye contact.

The Gorilla: not just a handshake, but a signal that says, "I can break you."

Try to find a happy medium—say, a giraffe, or whatever.

PUZZLE TIME

GLASSES AND BREAD PLATES

You've said your hellos and taken your seat, and are ready to claim your bread plate and water glass. Unfortunately, all of the place settings are so close to each other that you don't know what is yours.

Your first step to looking professional is to remember this:

GLASSES ARE ON YOUR RIGHT. BREAD PLATE IS ON YOUR LEFT.

If anyone tries to use your glass, tell them to read this book.

Alternatively, place the blame on yourself and use the line, "I already used that glass to rinse my retainer."

AN EASY WAY TO REMEMBER

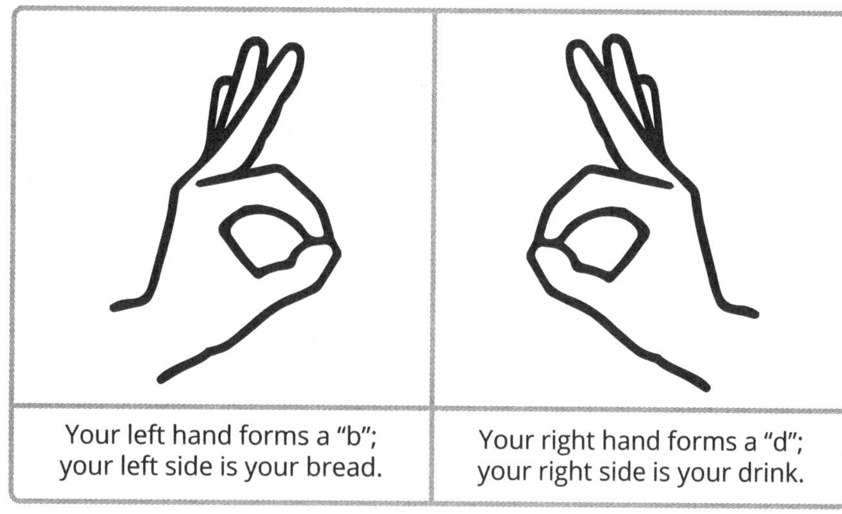

Your left hand forms a "b"; your left side is your bread.

Your right hand forms a "d"; your right side is your drink.

To help you remember where to find your bread plate and glasses, hold your hands out in front of you and make an old-fashioned "OK sign" with each.

Use a little imagination, and you'll see a "**b**" for "bread" and a "**d**" for "drink" on your left and right hands, respectively.

PLACING YOUR FOOD ORDER

OVERVIEW

Now it's time to order. You look at your menu and panic when you don't see words like "pizza." Ideally, you should never ask your server which dishes taste like chicken. We'll help you with this problem on the next page.

At this point in the meal, you're probably thinking one other thing when you look at the menu: *FREE*.

Yes, most business dinners mean free food for you. You'll be thinking, *What can I get away with?*

You'll probably order something that you don't usually try with your friends, but you still have to let good ol' Simon show you the way.

If Simon orders an appetizer, you should order an appetizer or a salad. Nothing is worse than watching a table of people eating. But if Simon gets only an entrée, you're probably out of luck ordering goose liver.

Speaking of goose liver, please see the following page.

THE MADE-TO-CONFUSE MENU

Restaurants go out of their way to disguise the true nature of some of their ingredients.

When you find out what all of these things actually are, you realize it makes sense for restaurants to use different names. It doesn't sound very appetizing to say,

> **"I'LL HAVE THE GOOSE LIVER AND FISH EGGS FOR MYSELF, AND PLEASE BRING SOME AIRSICKNESS BAGS FOR THE REST OF THE TABLE."**

bouillabaisse = fish stew

red mullet = fish, not a haircut

foie gras ("fwah grah") = goose liver

truffle = fungus

caviar = fish eggs

APPETIZERS

BOUILLABAISSE TERRINE — **$22.00**
with lobster, red mullet, dover sole, tomato and caviar

CHEF'S TRIO OF SOUP — **$23.00**
chicken with foie gras; pumpkin with prawns; fresh pea with goat cheese

GAME TERRINE — **$23.00**
of rabbit, venison, foie gras and squab with green apple truffle dressing

BELUGA CAVIAR SERVICE — **$65.00** per ounce

OTHER WORDS

The list is infinite, but here are a couple of other words that might pop up on a menu:

OTHER WORDS

CHILES	hot peppers
MORELS	brain-like fungus
RHUBARB	stalk of a plant (leaves are toxic)
VENISON	deer
CAPERS	flower bud
FRICASSEE	stew
TARTARE	raw
ESCARGOTS	snails
CEVICHE	raw fish
GNOCCHI	potato dumplings
VERMICELLI	thin spaghetti
ARUGULA	salad green
CARPACCIO	raw beef
LEEK	onion
TURBOT	fish
PARSNIP	root

SUSHI

If your work dinner takes you to a sushi restaurant, these are the basic things you'll need to know:

SUSHI
Raw fish (you'll have many choices) over rice is commonly referred to as sushi.

SASHIMI
This is raw fish without the rice.

ROLLS (MAKI)
Rolls are raw fish or some other food item (like cucumber) wrapped in rice and seaweed.

WASABI
Wasabi is a very spicy horseradish that looks like green Play-Doh (but it's certainly not child's play).

WHAT TO DO:
Add a little wasabi to the top of your maki. Using chopsticks, dip your food in the soy sauce and then your mouth. Chew. Swallow. Smile.

STEAK

Here's the part of the book that doesn't win points with vegetarians. But if you go out on a few work dinners, you'll inevitably wind up at a steakhouse.

When you go to a steakhouse, you already know what appears most on the menu: steak. But there is still plenty to decide. Steakhouses are famous for their variety of cuts of meat. This is what you need to know:

Meat is muscle. Unexercised muscle is tender. People like their meat tender.

Therefore, the best (and most expensive) pieces of meat come from the parts of the cow that are least exercised.

Take a look at the diagram on the following page.

MENU

FILET $23.95
Cut generously, broiled expertly to melt-in-your-mouth tenderness.

RIB EYE $23.50
Well-marbled for peak flavor, deliciously juicy.

PORTERHOUSE FOR TWO $25.95 /person
Combines the rich flavor of the strip with the tenderness of the filet.

TOFU STEAK $26.95
Maybe not, but you can always order some vegetarian sides.

CHUCK THE COW

This is Chuck, our friendly cow. Chuck never visits the gym. But he still gets exercise as he walks around all day eating grass. Therefore, the muscles around his legs are tough, whereas the short loin area (away from the legs) is most tender.

Now you're a cow expert.

Most steaks in a steakhouse come from the short loin (porterhouse, T-bone, filet, and NY strip).

STEAK MATH

What are the differences in the cuts? Surprisingly, many are alike. To see this, you'll have to do a little bit of "steak math."

T-BONE OR PORTERHOUSE = FILET + NY STRIP

RIB EYE = PRIME RIB

ONLY THE BEST

T-bone and porterhouse are each made up of two pieces of meat: a filet and a strip (one on each side of the bone). The porterhouse has a bigger filet than the T-bone.

Rib eye and prime rib are the same cuts of meat, just cooked differently. The rib eye is grilled while the prime rib is slow roasted.

If you remember one thing, remember that the filet mignon is usually the least exercised, most tender, and most expensive (per ounce) piece of meat. If you're out on the company bill and Simon leads you to the expensive side of the menu, give the filet a chance.

CHEWING THE CUD

Have you ever heard the expression "chewing the cud" when a number of people are sitting around talking about nothing? Have you ever wondered what that meant?

Apparently, cows have numerous stomachs. When a cow eats grass, it swallows its food into stomach number one. After a while, the cow *regurgitates* this food *back into its mouth*. The cow then re-eats this "grass" and swallows it again into a different stomach. That's disgusting. That's "chewing the cud."

Wait, maybe the expression is "chewing the fat." Anyway...

CLOSE YOUR MENU

Now back to the music. Up until now, things have been flowing pretty smoothly. You've got your drink, you've made up your mind about the food and appetizers, and you're ready to order.

One problem. You've got to:

CLOSE YOUR MENU!

It seems so obvious, but if you leave it open, the server is never going to come to your table.

When people start complaining about the service and then notice your menu still open, they're going to throw silverware at you.

OCEAN OF SILVER-WARE

SILVERWARE

When the food arrives, you're going to look down at your place setting and see an ocean of silverware before you. This diagram will help you navigate the high seas.

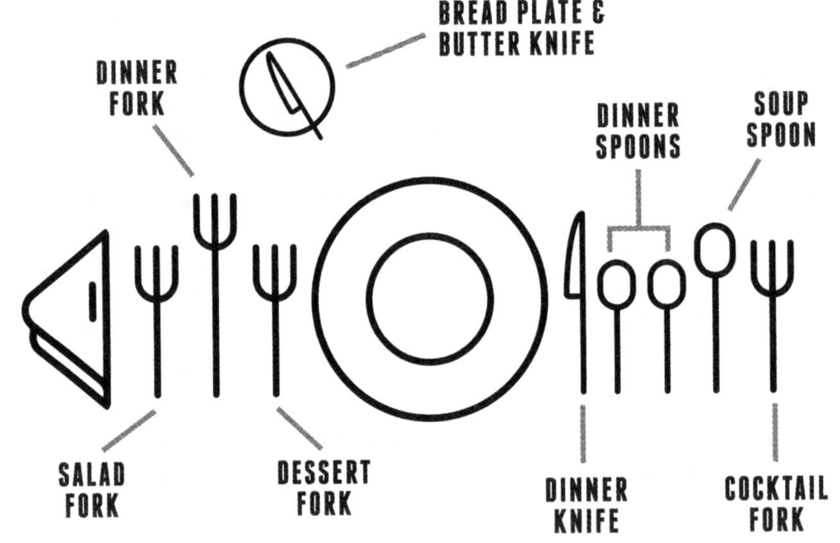

SILVERWARE REVIEW

When figuring out your silverware, here's your rule of thumb:

⟶ **WORK FROM THE OUTSIDE IN.**

The first courses will use the outer silverware.

Also, never allow used silverware to rest on the table. It should always be on your dish.

Also remember:

BUTTER KNIFE AND PLATE

You should always "butter your plate" first and use this butter for your bread. You want to avoid continually returning to the original butter. "Can you pass the butter... again...please?" is likely to get old.

BREAD

Tear off bite-sized portions of your bread, and butter only these portions as you eat them.

If you start the bread, offer the breadbasket to the person on your right and then pass the basket to your left. In general, *pass things to the left*.

SOUP SPOON AND BOWL

Your soup spoon is giant, because everyone should feel like an ogre eating porridge at least once in their life.

When you come to the bottom of your bowl, tilt the bowl away from you to get the last of your soup.

If you don't like your fellow diners, slurp as loudly as possible, belch, then turn to your neighbor and say, "Soup good. Me finished."

TEASPOONS

If you have two dinner spoons (as in the diagram on the page to the left), the outer spoon, not the inner spoon, is reserved for throwing. If you throw the inner spoon, you'll look foolish in front of everyone at the table. Actually, we can't find any good reason for a second spoon other than pretention.

BITE-SIZED PORTIONS

Make a conscious effort to eat bite-sized portions. Otherwise, you'll be forced into an uncomfortable 30-second pause when asked a question.

FINISHED EATING

FINISHED POSITION

Once you've finally finished eating, you should put your silverware on your plate, fork tines down, in this position (roughly 4 o'clock). Servers are actually trained to look for this.

In case you're wondering, they are also trained to ask you a question when your mouth is full.

AFTER DINNER

THANK YOU

Besides using manners, another way to distinguish yourself at a business dinner is to send a thank-you note to your host for inviting you to dinner.

This may not always be appropriate when the host was your immediate boss, but a thank-you is important if the host was a client. This simple gesture can go a long way.

REVIEW

The business dinner can be a very enjoyable experience if you remember the three most important rules:

YOU'RE NOT THERE TO EAT.
BE DISCREET.
FOLLOW THE LEAD OF YOUR HOST.

You're only at this meeting because Simon wants you there. Think of this as a compliment. Simon obviously likes you and wants you around. So relax and just be yourself.

BENEFITS

OVERVIEW

On your first day on the job, you may meet with someone from human resources to discuss your job benefits. If you're a rodeo clown, these benefits may include free face paint. For other jobs, you may get health insurance and extra money to put away for retirement.

Most of the discussion might include really boring words, like 401(k), HSA, HMO, PPO, and flex account. Flex what?

But here's the little secret: these benefits can be worth a lot of money to you. We'll share some tips so you can take advantage of them.

And if tips for free money aren't enough to get you interested, we'll even include a story about mermaids.

HEALTH INSURANCE

OVERVIEW

Until now, you've probably been covered by your parents' insurance plan. Once you graduate, you may need your own policy. In fact, many states kick you off your parents' insurance plan when you turn 26.

Health insurance is an important work benefit. If you don't have health insurance, something as minor as a broken arm could set you back thousands of dollars. A more serious condition could drain your bank account for years.

This section will give you a general overview of health insurance and the different plans available to you. The variations on each plan are nearly infinite.

The differences between some **HMOs** and **PPOs** can become one giant blur.

When you're offered insurance, take the time to read over your plan in detail. Ask a lot of questions.

The decisions you make now about insurance coverage are important, because unless you have a life event (marriage, the birth of a child, or divorce, for example) you cannot make changes until the next open enrollment. This typically happens in October and November.

You can't get sick and then say, "Ooh, ooh! I want the *good* plan now." They've figured that one out already.

OVERVIEW

Your employer will probably offer you its most cost-effective option. Occasionally, you may be allowed to upgrade your plan if you kick in some money of your own.

We'll walk through your different options and explain the standard plans. Before we do, here are some of the words you'll encounter in virtually every plan.

Most plans use the same jargon.

INSURANCE JARGON

DEDUCTIBLE

The dollar amount (usually per calendar year) you need to pay out of pocket for medical expenses before the insurance kicks in.

CO-PAYMENT

A small fee (often $5 to $20) you pay every time you visit a doctor.

PREMIUM

Your monthly payment for insurance coverage. Your employer may pay some of your premium.

PAYABLE IN POP-TARTS

If you see this expression in an insurance document, something is wrong.

PCP

Primary care physician: the family doctor you often need to contact before you can see a specialist. Often referred to as a "gatekeeper."

OUT-OF-POCKET MAXIMUM

The most money you'll have to pay in a calendar year for "reasonable" and "customary" care. Your insurance will pick up the costs above this amount.

PREEXISTING CONDITION

This requirement to disclose your allergy to whale blubber can actually help you when you end up in an emergency room and the doctors contact your insurer for information about your medical history.

OVERVIEW

STANDARD HMO

HEALTH MAINTENANCE ORGANIZATION

You have to contact your primary care physician (PCP) first before you see anyone else.

To the left is your basic health plan, the standard **HMO**. Of the plans we cover, it's usually the least expensive and the least flexible.

When you sign up with an HMO, your insurance company will grant you access to their website. This is where you will find a registry of doctors approved by the plan. These are called your **IN-NETWORK** doctors. If you visit any doctors outside of this network, you're on your own when paying the bill (except for emergencies).

Imagine you are a mermaid (or merman) and want to remove your tail. You'll lower your chances of winning the 400-meter freestyle, but riding a bicycle will be easier.

MERMAID PROBLEMS

Your local drug store doesn't carry mermaid tail removal cream, so you need to see a specialist.

If you were part of an HMO, the best mermaid tail removal specialist in the country, Dr. Tailbegone, might not be in your network. For your insurance company to pick up some of the cost, you might have to use a local specialist (Dr. Chopitov) who has worked only on a few mermaids.

You could still go to Dr. Tailbegone, but you'd have to pay the entire bill yourself. For this reason, a network is often unpopular, since you're restricted as to what doctors you can visit under the plan.

The standard HMO has another restriction. Within this network of doctors, you're required to pick one as your main doctor (usually a family doctor). We'll call this doctor "Dr. Friendly."

Dr. Friendly is your **PCP**, or **PRIMARY CARE PHYSICIAN**. If you get sick, you go to Dr. Friendly first. If you sprain your ankle, you go to Dr. Friendly. If you get a pencil stuck in your ear, you see Dr. Friendly.

So, what's the problem? When Dr. Friendly gives you a shot, you get a lollipop, right?

The problem is that you always have to contact Dr. Friendly before you can see Dr. Skin, Dr. Nose, or Dr. Tailbegone. Your insurance will not cover visits to any other doctors unless you have a referral from Dr. Friendly. (There are a few exceptions, like emergencies.)

STANDARD HMO SUMMARY:

- LESS EXPENSIVE
- LESS FLEXIBLE
- YOU MUST CONTACT YOUR PCP EVERY TIME
- YOU MUST STAY IN-NETWORK

OVERVIEW

STANDARD PPO

PREFERRED PROVIDER ORGANIZATION

You can go to any doctor you want OR go in-network for less money.

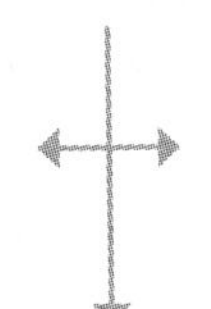

A **PPO** is often your most flexible plan, but also the most expensive.

Under a PPO, you don't *have* to choose one main doctor. (There's no requirement to see Dr. Friendly, that is, no PCP.) This means that if you need to get an unwanted tail removed, you can go directly to Dr. Tailbegone without getting permission from anyone else.

Your insurance company will still provide you with a list of doctors. But this time, if you go to a doctor outside the network, your insurance company will help you pay for some of the bill. You'll have more flexibility.

Of course, if you choose from within your network, you'll pay less of the bill, but at least your insurance company will pay some of the costs for out-of-network doctors.

OVERVIEW

As you can see in the diagram on the right, you might pay 40% of the costs if you use a doctor outside your network, but you'll pay only 10% if you stay in-network.

If you are really concerned about which doctors you would go to in case of a serious accident or illness, then a PPO will give you the greatest flexibility.

STANDARD PPO SUMMARY:

- EXPENSIVE, BUT FLEXIBLE
- YOU HAVE NO PCP TO VISIT
- YOU CAN GO IN- OR OUT-OF-NETWORK

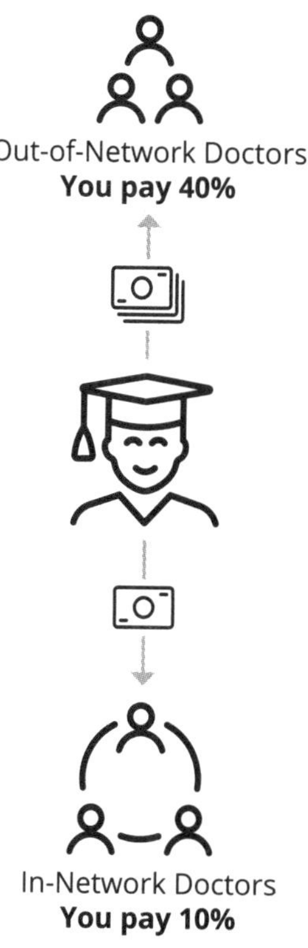

GET FRIENDLY

When you move, you not only get new friends and a new grocery store, but you get a new doctor as well. Many people forget this.

When you move or start a new health insurance plan, immediately get to know your new "Dr. Friendly" (**PCP**/general physician). Start your relationship early.

We know this can be difficult, but consider making an appointment for a general physical with your new doctor.

Call your old doctor and get your health records forwarded. It is better to do this now when you are feeling fine than to wait until you are a flu-ridden, sniveling mess in need of medicine.

STANDARD POS

POINT OF SERVICE PLAN

OVERVIEW

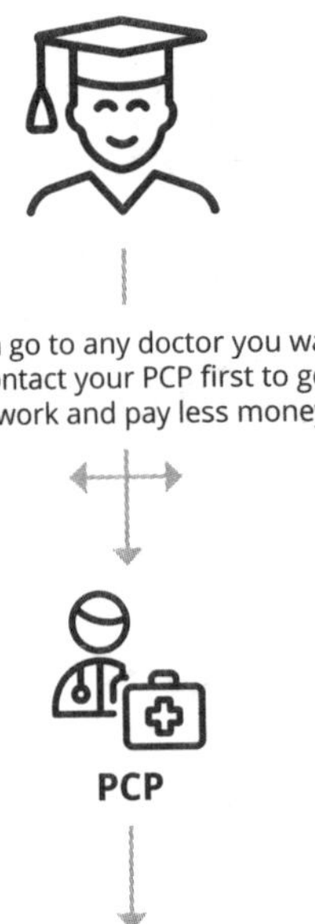

An infinite variety of plans fall between an HMO and a PPO. Here is an example of one **POINT OF SERVICE (POS)** plan.

As you can see from the diagram on the next page, a POS is part HMO, part PPO.

PART HMO:

You still have Dr. Friendly (PCP) to deal with before you can go to any of the in-network doctors.

PART PPO:

You still have the flexibility to see any doctor outside your network, for an added cost.

STANDARD POS SUMMARY:

- MODERATE PRICE AND FLEXIBILITY
- MUST VISIT YOUR PCP FOR IN-NETWORK CARE
- YOU CAN GO IN- OR OUT-OF-NETWORK

REVIEW OF STANDARD HEALTH INSURANCE PLANS

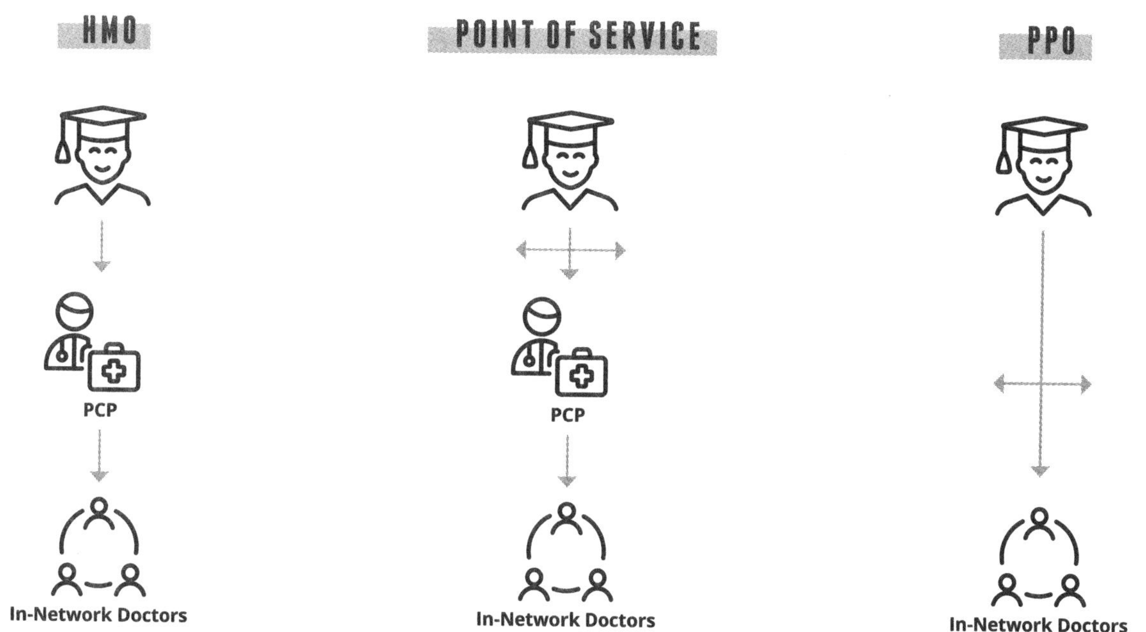

MORE FLEXIBILITY, HIGHER PRICE

MAKE YOUR CHOICE

You've been presented with a number of choices. Which is best for you?

To start, your employer may offer you a certain plan (usually of the HMO variety) as part of your employment. You may have the option to upgrade your plan.

If you are prone to sickness or concerned that you may need the best specialist in the event of an emergency, you may want to consider a more comprehensive plan, like a PPO.

An HMO might be a good choice if you are on a tight budget and aren't as concerned about your coverage.

Remember, you can usually change your plan only during the open enrollment period, so try to be very selective about your choices now.

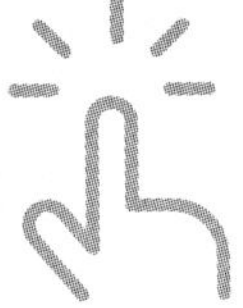

SHORT-TERM COVERAGE

Your employer may not offer you health insurance until you've been on the job for three months or sometimes may not offer it at all.

You may think to yourself, "Nothing is going to happen." Not surprisingly, the mysterious forces behind Murphy's Law seem to activate themselves during gaps in insurance coverage.

Fortunately, you can get short-term coverage for up to six months while you're in between coverages.

Short-term insurance is intended to cover you in the event of an **emergency**, like an unexpected visit to the ER.

The premiums, or monthly payments, are usually **cheaper** than premiums for normal health insurance.

It's usually **easier** to get short-term coverage. The provider will usually not ask you as many questions about your health.

Your deductible is **per incident or illness**. Most long-term plans will have a deductible for the year, but short-term coverage is per incident. Each incident will cost you money out of your pocket.

If you're not offered insurance at a new job, you can sometimes purchase the same insurance offered by your previous employer (if you had one) for up to 18 months. (This is called **COBRA**.)

THE 401(K)

THE GREATEST PERK

OVERVIEW

You've probably heard the term "401(k)." But like that poem in high school, you're not quite sure what it actually means.

Put simply, a 401(k) is a company-sponsored plan that allows you to save your money (just as you normally would), but with a bunch of added perks.

Why the odd name? Well, the government wanted a name that was vague and uninformative, yet still difficult to remember. It's their way of reminding you not to judge a book by its cover.

Despite the name, a 401(k) (or a 403(b), which is basically the same thing) is a great perk to take advantage of if your employer offers it.

On your first day of work, you may be asked what percentage of your paycheck you'd like to invest in your 401(k).

You are allowed to take a certain dollar amount per year and invest this money in different mutual fund choices provided by your employer.

A 401(k) is not an investment itself, but more like a "special box" for you to wrap your investments in, topped with a nice little bow. This box is special, because it allows your money to grow tax-free until you take it out. When money grows tax-free, it grows faster than a taxed investment does. Here's another nice benefit of a 401(k):

IT'S GOOD FOR THOSE OF YOU WITH NO SELF-CONTROL.

OVERVIEW

Since the money comes out of your paycheck before you even see it, no harm is done. This is an opportunity for you to save your money without having to be aware of how many dinners out you're sacrificing.

If you have a tendency to order filet mignon over ramen every night, a 401(k)'s built-in self-control will work wonders for you.

DRAWBACKS

Unfortunately, with few exceptions, you can't take your money out of a 401(k) until you're 59½ (at which time, it will get taxed). That's why it's usually called a retirement account.

That being said, you shouldn't think of a 401(k) just as a retirement account, because that might make you feel sad and old inside.

Think of it more as a birthday present to yourself for turning 60. That way, you will be able to say,

"HI, SELF, HAPPY BIRTHDAY. LOOK WHAT I GOT YOU. IT'S ENOUGH MONEY TO LIVE ON FOR THE REST OF YOUR LIFE. WASN'T THAT THOUGHTFUL OF ME?"

Why worry about saving for retirement now? Surprisingly, worrying now will make a *big* difference later. And you can even get a head start on those wrinkles!

ALEX VS. DUNCE

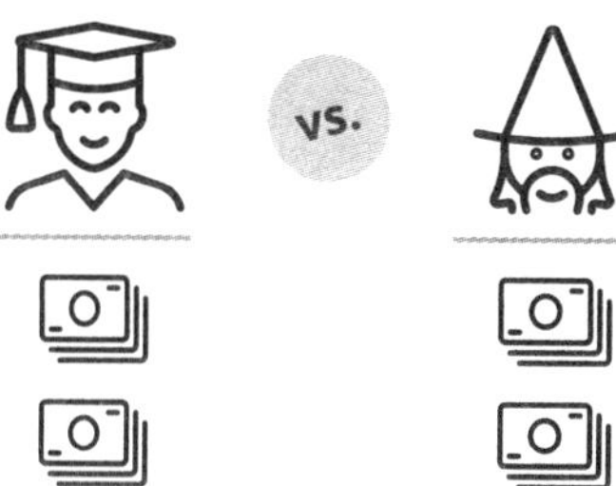

Consider this example. Alex puts $2,000 into a retirement account (or any investment, for that matter) at age 25, and then again at age 26, and does this every year until age 35. At this point Alex stops investing and leaves the funds in the account to earn interest.

Dunce (based on the name, you can probably see where this is going) doesn't start saving until age 35. To make up for lost time, Dunce adds $2,000 every year for 30 years.

ALEX VS. DUNCE — THE RESULTS ARE IN

Now assume each account earns 10% every year. This is a big assumption, but it's possible. Plus it illustrates the following point.

Who is going to have more money at age 65: Alex with 10 years or Dunce with 30?

Take a look at this graph. Alex wins by a landslide. He can now fill a bathtub with bills. Why?

COMPOUND INTEREST.

The interest on Alex's early investment compounds so fast that Dunce can never catch up. Dunce can fill a bathtub only with nickels.

If you don't believe this simple graph (thanks for the trust), take a look at the numbers on the next page.

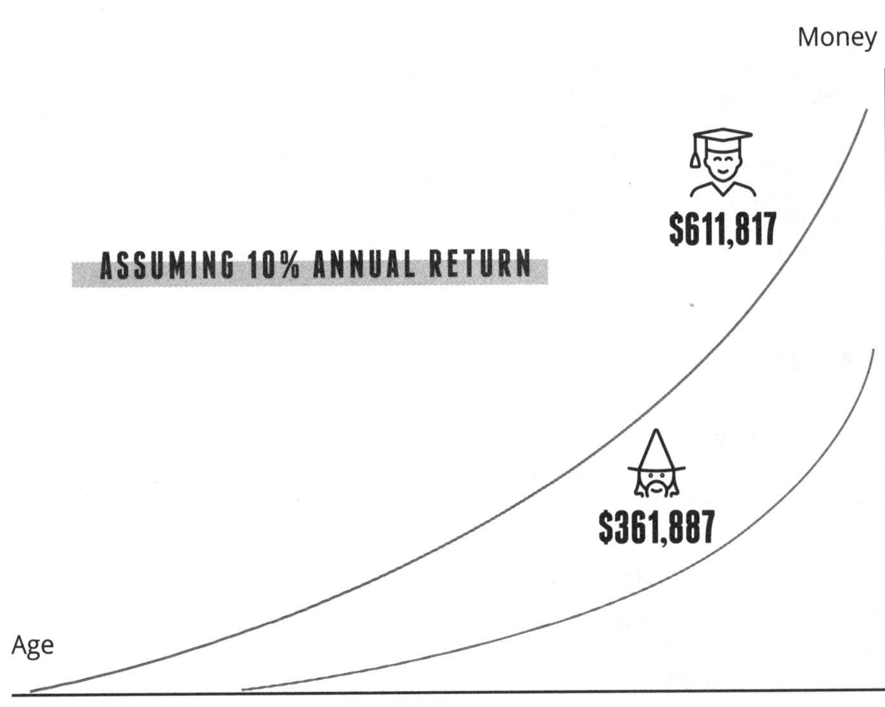

ALEX VS. DUNCE: BEHIND THE SCENES

Alex contributes $2,000 annually from age 25 to 35.

ALEX'S 401(K) INCREASES BY $7,516 IN INTEREST OVER ONE YEAR.

The power of Alex's interest overwhelms Dunce's late start into the race.

AGE	ALEX'S 401(K)	ALEX ADDS	DUNCE'S 401(K)	DUNCE ADDS
40	$56,468	$0	$15,431	$2,000
41	$62,115	$0	$18,974	$2,000
42	$68,327	$0	$22,872	$2,000
43	$75,159	$0	$27,159	$2,000
44	$82,675	$0	$31,875	$2,000
45	$90,943	$0	$37,062	$2,000
46	$100,037	$0	$42,769	$2,000
47	$110,041	$0	$49,045	$2,000
48	$121,045	$0	$55,950	$2,000
49	$133,149	$0	$63,545	$2,000
50	$146,464	$0	$71,899	$2,000

Dunce contributes $2,000 annually from age 35 to 65.

Dunce makes:

$ 2,716 IN INTEREST + $ 2,000 OF HIS MONEY INVESTED

$ 4,716 OVER ONE YEAR

Mathlete fact: They'd "tie" at age 65 if the compound rate were 6.25% instead of 10%. Still surprising.

MATCHED 401(K)

OVERVIEW

To make a 401(k) even better, sometimes your company will offer a perk called a 401(k) **MATCH**.

Translation: your company will "match" (or some percentage of that amount) the amount of money you put into your 401(k) every year. If you add $100, they'll add $100, with no strings attached. (That's a 100% return.) The company is essentially giving you a raise without any work on your part (the best kind of raise).

There will often be a limit imposed on the match. For example, your company may match only up to 3% of your salary. But who cares? This is free money.

Look at the graph below. When you compare this investment to other "no-risk" investments (or any other investments, for that matter), it has a great return.

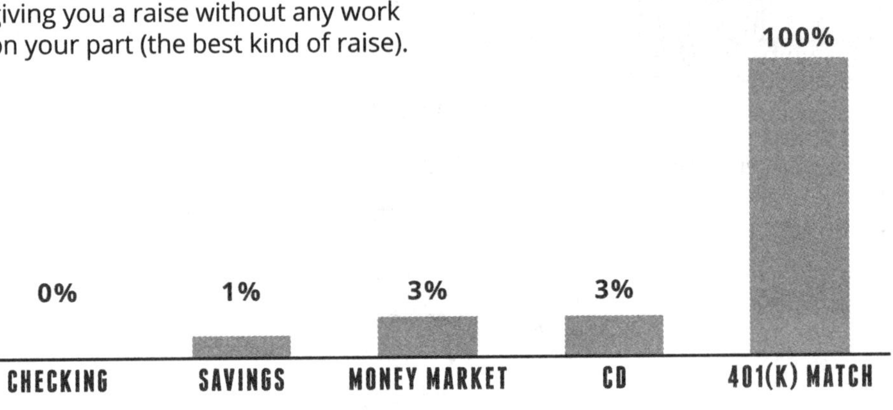

FLEX ACCOUNTS

WHAT'S A FLEX ACCOUNT?

Many employers offer flexible spending accounts, or **FLEX ACCOUNTS**, as a benefit. However, most people do not know what these are for or how to take advantage of them.

A FLEX ACCOUNT IS THE EQUIVALENT OF A BIG "DISCOUNT STICKER" ON YOUR MEDICAL BILLS.

On your first day on the job, your human resources rep will ask you how much you'd like to put in your flex account. Let's assume you say, "$1,000." Your employer will divide this $1,000 by the number of paychecks left in the year. If there are 20, then $50 will be deducted from each of the next 20 paychecks.

When this money is deducted from your paycheck, Uncle Sam never gets the chance to take any of it. You pay no taxes on it. The money is transferred directly from your salary into this account. (This deal is no longer exclusively for mobsters.)

Say you have a medical expense, like a prescription refill. You will have a "co-pay" at the pharmacy. You can use the money in your flex account to cover this co-pay.

Normally you would have paid for it out of your pocket. Now your flex account pays for it, and you are the coolest person in the office.

A flex account is like a discount sticker, because you are using money that has never been taxed.

FLEX ACCOUNT

A flex account is great, so what's the catch?

IF YOU DON'T USE IT, YOU LOSE IT.

If you don't spend your $1,000 by the end of the year, you lose your money.

That said, you should ask your HR representative exactly what medical expenses you are permitted to pay with your flex account.

Then figure out how much money you spend on contact lenses, glasses, and doctor's visits over a year. Contribute only the amount you think you'll spend.

YOUR OPTIONS

If flex accounts still don't make any sense, look at the diagram to the right.

Let's assume you get $100 in salary.

In option 1 (**no flex account**), you have **$70** to pay for medical expenses, because you pay $30 in taxes to Uncle Sam.

In option 2 (**flex account**), you have **$100** to pay for medical expenses, because you don't pay taxes to Uncle Sam.

$100 is more than $70, so use a flex account when you can.

TWO OPTIONS WHEN PAYING MEDICAL EXPENSES

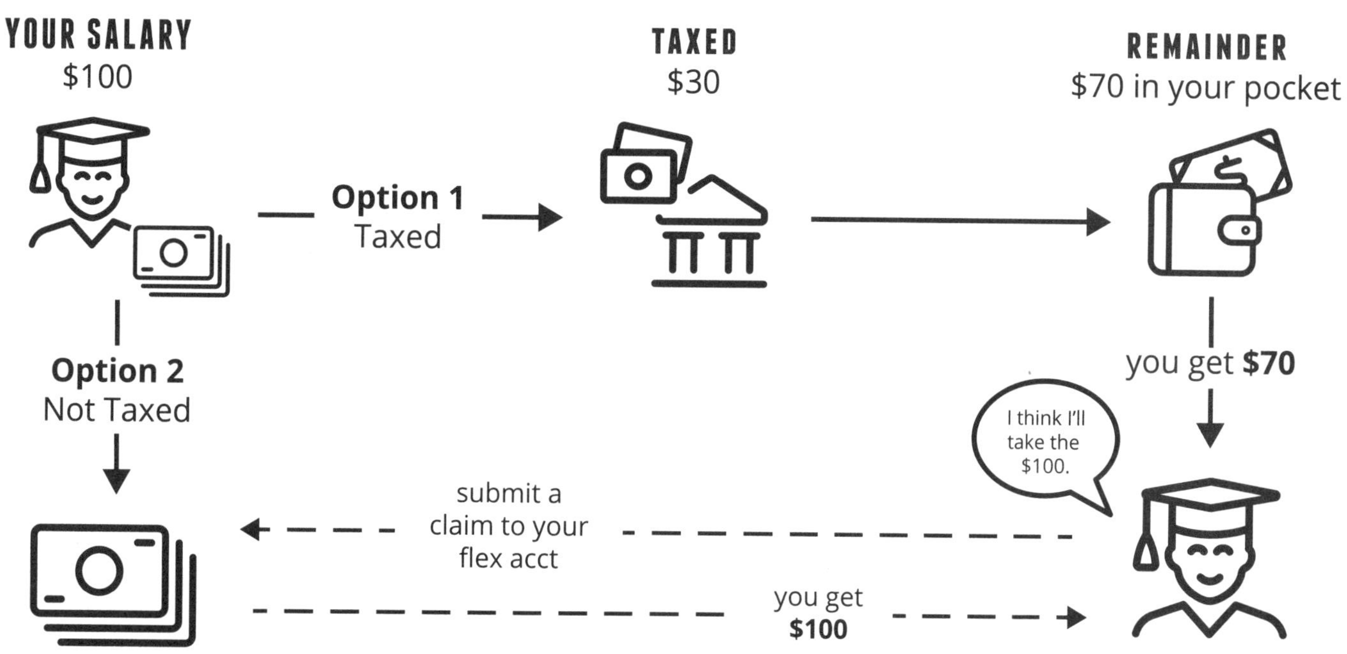

HEALTH SAVINGS ACCOUNTS

OVERVIEW

If you're young and healthy, you may opt to spend less money (lower premium) by taking a high-deductible plan, which is often eligible for a health savings account, or **HSA**. Since this gem is a great way to save money, we'll tell you how it works.

SET IT UP

Confirm that you're getting an "HSA-compatible" insurance plan. Then do an online search for banks that offer HSA accounts. This checking account doesn't have to be affiliated with your insurance company.

FUND YOUR HSA ACCOUNT

You can deposit up to a maximum of roughly $3,000 (for an individual) in your HSA checking account. If you contribute more money than you spend in a year, your money stays in your account for the next year. (You don't lose it as with a flex account.)

SPEND

Use checks or your debit card to spend money from your account on a large range of allowable medical expenses (including some that your insurance doesn't even cover). The list includes co-pays, prescription and over-the-counter drugs (like allergy medication), dental and vision care, and much more. In most cases, you can't use your account to pay for your insurance premiums.

OVERVIEW

THE BENEFITS

You indirectly save 10% to 35% on the medical expenses that you have paid from your HSA account.

WHY?

In April, when you file your taxes, you'll be able to take a deduction (see our topic on **TAXES**) for the money you deposited into your HSA. This benefit could save you hundreds of dollars every year.

TWO PARTS TO AN HSA

EMPLOYMENT

EMPLOYMENT

As you may have discovered in the **BUSINESS DINNERS** section, there's a lot more to the job than just the work. Your communication with colleagues and how you present yourself are also important.

You'll spend a lot of hours at work, so we'll share tips on interviewing, email etiquette, remote work, staying connected, and more to keep you happy and successful.

To pique your interest, we'll also cover

- scary clowns
- vague emails
- body odor
- voiceless robots
- pajamas
- Judge Judy

JOB INTER-VIEW

INTERVIEW PREP

You got a job interview. Congrats! Now let's get you the job.

An interview helps a company to decide if it should invest real money in you. By preparing well, you tell the company that you're a serious candidate worthy of its investment.

GET LOCAL FEEDBACK

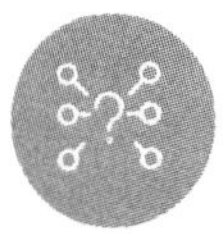

Use LinkedIn or your alumni network to locate someone in the company to call prior to your interview. Ask about company culture and your position.

"But that's scary," you say. No, clowns are scary. When you mention this call in your interview, you'll sound awesome.

RESEARCH QUESTIONS

Anticipate what you'll be asked by searching the web for common interview questions. You might get asked about strengths and weaknesses, past challenges, or the coefficient of linear thermal expansion for stainless steel (depending on the position).

PREPARE QUESTIONS

Research the company and prepare good questions to ask your interviewers. "No, I think you answered everything" is secret company code for "I'm not very interested in this job."

PRACTICE

Run through mock interviews with family, friends, or career center.

INTERVIEW DAY

DRESS WELL

Find out about the company dress code and dress accordingly. Interview outfits should be professional, comfortable, and entirely forgettable to your interviewer.

INTERVIEW

Now that you're prepared, you have two big goals in the interview:

1. To show you're qualified.

2. To show you're interested.

ARRIVE EARLY

Expect a traffic jam, a hailstorm, and, for good measure, a flat tire. If you get lucky, you'll arrive at the interview an hour early. Hang out in your car and call your friend or family.

RELAX

Since you're prepared and not rushed, you'll be able to relax in your interview. Turn off your phone to avoid notifications and don't fidget.

DISPLAY GOOD BODY LANGUAGE

Give a firm handshake and make good eye contact.

ASK QUESTIONS

Now is the time to separate yourself from the pack. Ask your prepared questions. Discuss the call(s) you made to current employees. Don't ask questions for the sake of asking questions—learn about the company. Is this the right job for you?

BE GENUINE

No one likes the person who answers, "My biggest weakness is that I have no weaknesses." If you're honest and authentic, your interviewer will get to know you (and not harbor lingering doubts).

AFTER THE INTERVIEW

PREPARE FOR THE FOLLOW-UP

Ask about the next steps. ***When will you hear back?*** Request a business card so you can follow up.

EMAIL

Send a brief thank-you email within 24 hours of your interview.

WRITTEN FOLLOW-UP

Your interviewer wants to know if you really want the job (and maybe you don't). Send a *handwritten* card to stand out from other applicants.

DON'T TWEET ABOUT IT

If you're big into social media, don't post about your interview. Assume they're following you on the web (and possibly in real life, if you've applied to the CIA).

WORK ETIQUETTE

OVERVIEW

You got the job. Congrats! Now what?

We did some informal polling of companies that hire a lot of new college graduates. Where could your new hires improve?

These next few columns provide some inside scoop. Between these tips and your charming personality, you'll be CEO of the company in no time at all.

PERSONAL TOUCH

Alex, this book's protagonist, received a brief email from their boss: "That's nice."

"'That's nice'? Was that a compliment, or is she just patronizing me? Yes, she might be more senior than me, but I'm really smart. 'That's nice.' Who does she think she is?"

How can something as harmless as "That's nice" in an email send someone into a tizzy?

Email, chat, and texting just don't do a good job of capturing the nuances of conversation, like voice inflection and body language.

PERSONAL TOUCH

Instead of using emoticons to bridge the gap, focus on more in-person or verbal communications on the job.

If someone asks for a "live" meeting, give them a live meeting. A voicemail should be returned with a voicemail or live meeting, but never with an email or text.

Over the past few years, the biggest complaint that we've heard from companies about college new hires is their **overuse of technology in communication**.

Show your new colleagues your amazing personality and communication skills. Walk over to their desks and show them your pearly whites instead of sending them an email.

RESPONDING

After the lack of personal touch, the second biggest complaint from employers concerns the *responsiveness* of post-college new hires.

Be timely. You look professional when you reply to a request quickly at work. Never let 24 hours go by without at least acknowledging a request or question.

No response. If you're unable to do something or be somewhere, it's OK to respond with a no. You lose points when you *never* respond to a request or question in the workplace.

BLOGS

Since Alex knows they're the center of the universe, they post weekly messages on their blog about their favorite TV show and cereal.

After the huge "That's nice" email drama, Alex wrote some not-so-nice comments about their boss on their blog. Since no one at work ever reads it, Alex didn't think it would be a problem, until someone did.

After a meeting with their human resources representative, Alex learned about their company's strict public blogging policies. "It's a free country, but your employer is free to fire you, too," Alex later wrote.

If your blog mentions work, get permission. Or, just be smart and complain to your roommate instead.

EMAIL ETIQUETTE

Your friends might enjoy your crazy Santa hat smiley face in emails, but email rules change once you're on the job.

GET TO THE POINT

Keep your emails brief, avoid long sentences and paragraphs, and try to answer questions before they are asked.

CHOOSE A GOOD SUBJECT

If your boss gets 300 emails a day and you don't include a subject line in your email, you might inadvertently make your message less of a priority. A subject line will also make it easier to search through emails.

FONTS

As the philosopher Plato once said, "An email font is the window to your soul, so choose wisely." If the decision is yours, use Times New Roman to say, "I conform." Verdana tells people that you're trying to be different in that non-Harley-Davidson kind of way. Kristin ITC suggests that you'd rather be eating ice cream.

EMPHASIS

Don't overuse the high priority option, and nothing deserves four exclamation points!!!! Plus, too many exclamation points can trigger email spam filters.

PROOFREAD

As thoughts flow out of your head, they inevitably stumble a few times as they come out of your fingers. Always reread your emails before sending them. Spellcheck will not pick up errors such as "Did you like my massage?"

CAPITALIZATION

Everyone loves free expression, but for business emails, keep your inner artist away from the caps lock key. capitalize the beginning of each sentence, and DON'T SCREAM WITH ALL CAPS.

EMAIL ETIQUETTE

PERSONAL USE

When you quickly hide your phone every time your boss visits your desk, it's obvious that you're on Instagram or Facebook. Do the personal stuff on your watch.

ATTACHMENTS

Keep them small. Big ones are annoying, because they take forever to download.

REPLY ALL

Everyone in your office does not need to know your every thought, so use "reply all" sparingly. And everyone hates the person who uses "reply all" to get removed from a group email.

PLAY IT SAFE

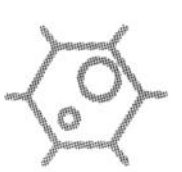

An offensive or obscene email never goes away. A computer virus downloaded from your personal email account can affect everyone in the office. Be thoughtful with your email use at work.

THE WORKSPACE

KEEP YOUR AREA PROFESSIONAL

Whether you want it to be or not, your workspace is a reflection of you.

LIMIT PERSONAL PHONE USE

No one around you wants to hear you scheduling fun weekend hangouts with your friends while you're supposed to be working. Know what kind of phone use is permitted and follow those guidelines.

THE WORKSPACE

KEEP YOUR CELL PHONE ON SILENT

Not everyone likes your ringtone as much as you do, and the sounds of new notifications are a distraction to you and others.

BE MINDFUL OF ODORS

If you don't have your own office, your colleagues will be stuck smelling your perfume, cologne, or yesterday's breakfast.

GENERAL TIPS

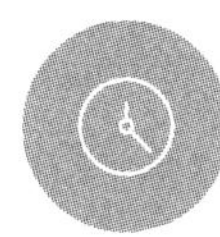

ARRIVE EARLY

You'll quickly gain a poor reputation if you continually show up late, especially for meetings. Get there five minutes early.

DRESS APPROPRIATELY

This will depend on your job and workplace, but make sure you are dressed at least as nicely as your colleagues. Know the dress code and adhere to it.

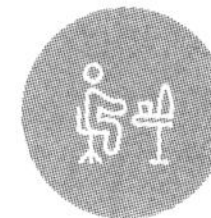

RESPECT SHARED SPACES

Don't leave a mess in the kitchen, bathroom, or other communal areas.

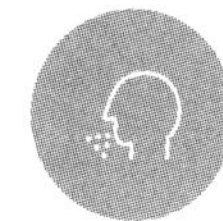

STAY HOME IF YOU ARE SICK

Don't come in to work if you're contagious with something. You may fall behind taking sick days, but no one wants to catch your sickness.

REMOTE WORK

STAY CONNECTED

If you're not working in a physical office, you won't see your coworkers around the water cooler. So make an extra effort to stay connected.

ASK QUESTIONS

Your coworkers know things. Reach out with questions, ask for feedback, or communicate concerns about a particular project.

EMBRACE PHONE CALLS

You don't need to be a voiceless robot typing into the void. Remind coworkers that you are a real person by giving them a call to discuss the latest project. And if you are indeed a robot, you should still call them and try to pass the Turing test.

SHARE SIMILAR WORK SCHEDULES

You'll stay more connected if you and your coworkers work at the same time. So if you choose to work at 2:00 a.m. every day, make sure to give your coworkers a friendly wake-up call before you log on (wink).

BE AVAILABLE

Let your coworkers know that you're open to phone calls, messages, and pizza deliveries.

STAY HAPPY

If you're happy and you know it (when working remotely), clap your hands!

PRIORITIZE YOUR SOCIAL ACTIVITIES

Be intentional about joining local groups or organizations.

GET OUT OF THE HOUSE EVERY DAY

Go for a walk, see other humans, and get some fresh air. Even sticking your head out of your bedroom window is a good start.

CHANGE CLOTHES

You'll be tempted to wear pajamas all day, every day. It's understandable. But you'll feel better about yourself if you maintain at least a semi-decent outer appearance.

SPEND TIME AROUND OTHERS

Engage in your hobbies. Do something fun. Having work-life balance is still crucial when you are working remotely, just as it would be if you were working in an office.

VALIDATE YOURSELF

You may hear that remote work isn't "real work." You bet it's real work! Just because you're still in your pajamas (despite our advice) doesn't mean you aren't a productive and valuable member of society.

STAY PRODUCTIVE

KEEP YOUR WORK AND PERSONAL SPACES SEPARATE

If you work in your bedroom, you might think about sleeping too much. Invest in a desk. For a few bucks, you can increase your moneymaking power tenfold.

CHUNK YOUR TASKS

Group different types of work together (email, reviewing docs, etc.) so you can focus.

MAINTAIN A SCHEDULE

It can be difficult to find motivation while working remotely, but creating a routine and forcing yourself to sit down and work at certain times will keep you accountable.

AVOID FORESEEABLE DISTRACTIONS

Maybe you need to shut the door to your work space to keep pets out, or politely ask roommates not to bother you for a certain amount of time.

COFFEE SHOPS

Occasionally, work in a coffee shop. The Hawthorne effect claims that you may work better when you're being observed. Plus, a change of scenery and a sugary coffee drink can be good for the soul (though maybe not for the body).

But a good *coffee* shop doesn't mean a good *work* spot. Consider its internet, typical customers, comfortable chairs, available chairs, and power outlets. If most of these factors are bad, the coffee shop probably doesn't want you working there for hours.

BEWARE OF PUBLIC WI-FI

Make sure to use a virtual private network (VPN). This creates a super-secret tunnel for your data to come and go so bad people don't steal your passwords. Even if you're not a computer nerd, search your app store or the web for good VPNs.

If the internet is spotty, get a mobile hotspot (Mi-Fi). This device talks to the internet and gives your computer reliable internet. Alternatively, you can create a hotspot from your phone, but you might use up your data and battery.

BE RESPECTFUL

Be mindful of your volume on video calls, how much space you take up, and how long you stay. A good coffee shop for remote working will let you stay all day, but you should order something—and tip the staff!—every couple of hours. Remember, the coffee shop is a business.

BRING NOISE-CANCELLING HEADPHONES

Instead of becoming irate when the happy couple at the next table has a loud conversation, recognize that this is an unavoidable side effect of working in public and pop on your headphones.

UNEMPLOYMENT

OVERVIEW

When you meet someone for the first time, you'll usually get the question

"SO, WHAT DO YOU DO?"

within the first 30 seconds.

If you're unemployed, it's no fun to answer that question. In fact, being unemployed is one of the most stressful experiences in life. Think of the tips below as a literary massage.

NO JUDGE JUDY

If you find yourself watching daytime television by yourself day after day, you'll go crazy. Get out of your house and do something. Anything.

TIPS

EGO

Remember that you're not what you do (unless you're an anteater). Your ego may take a bruising if you are laid off, but you should frequently look at yourself in the mirror and say, "Wow, you're really good-looking. Would you like pancakes?" Of course you would.

GO CHEAP

Plan on being unemployed for a while (but let's hope not). Cut expenses. Seek out free events and free stuff around town.

FIND A TEMPORARY JOB

If possible, try to nab something temporary while you look for something more long-term. The schedule and productivity will make you happier, and you'll feel more secure with a source of income.

UNEMPLOYMENT INSURANCE

If you're eligible, you can generally receive unemployment benefits for a few months after a layoff.

OPPORTUNITY

What do you want to do when you grow up? You may get an idea for a new career by freelancing, volunteering, or even browsing through specialty books in a bookstore or online. Search your almighty soul for that career that you'd actually like to get up for in the morning. And if that ideal job doesn't occur to you after a good soul search, don't fret! Take things one day at a time and keep an open mind.

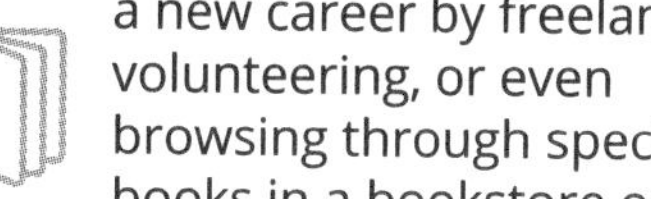

USE YOUR RESOURCES

Schedule lunches with friends; utilize the career resources from your alma mater; use online social networks for leads; or contact a job agency. Reach out to acquaintances who might know of an opportunity, especially since they may be able to talk to someone hiring and tell them positive things about you. Good jobs usually don't come from Craigslist.

STAY PROACTIVE

Interview, interview, interview and keep your résumé current. If all else fails, be nice to people. Someone might be nice back with a great job lead.

SECTION TWO:

LIFE

Tristan's gym contract got out of hand.

HAPPINESS

DAILY HAPPINESS

Over the past few years, a bunch of smart people have spent time studying the science of happiness. After reading a fair amount of "happiness research" (start with an online search—it's interesting), we're really happy (ha ha ha ha!) to share our findings with you.

To start, we all have a highly resilient "baseline" happiness level. People who suffer great losses or great gains quickly return to their baseline level.

With that said, what makes people happy? Make your guesses before you start the next page.

DAILY HAPPINESS

STAYING BUSY

Yep, staying busy helps. When you're engaged in an activity, rather than passively watching Netflix, you tend to be happier.

SPIRITUALITY

No single religion claims the happiness trophy, but "spiritual" people tend to be happier.

CHILDREN

Nope. Surprisingly, there is little correlation between happiness and parenthood. Statistically speaking, kids might make you feel more comfortable speaking about poop in public, but they won't make you more or less happy.

MONEY

Maybe. If your financial situation has you worried about food and shelter, more money will make you happy. But once your basic needs are met, more money will typically lead to only small, temporary increases in happiness.

HEALTHY RELATIONSHIPS

Ding! Across almost every study, the best predictor of happiness is healthy relationships with family and friends, particularly satisfying marriages or lifelong partnerships.

BE NICE

WAYS TO BE NICE

Why be nice? For starters, *you'll* feel nice. More important, *they'll* feel nice and might be nice to *someone else*. Niceness is contagious.

GREET STRANGERS

Say "good morning" with a smile as you pass people on the sidewalk. This phrase is most effective during the morning hours.

PAY FOR A STRANGER'S COFFEE

When you're in a Starbucks drive-thru, pay an extra $5 for the order of the person behind you. They'll talk about this act of kindness all day.

GIVE A COMPLIMENT

Most people think about what they put on in the morning. Tell them you like their shoes or shirt, and they'll probably smile.

REACH OUT FIRST

Your friends and family want to call you, but they may be distracted with life. Call them first and make their day.

LISTEN

Don't talk about yourself, but listen to someone else's story with focus. Then ask them a follow-up question.

MORE WAYS TO BE NICE

REMEMBER SOMEONE'S NAME

For someone you often see but don't know well, learn their name. Then say, "Hi, Jane." Unless their name is John. Then say, "Hi, John."

BRING TREATS TO WORK

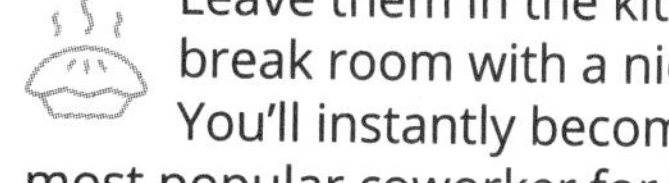

Leave them in the kitchen or break room with a nice note. You'll instantly become the most popular coworker for the day.

WRITE A POSITIVE ONLINE REVIEW

Small businesses will appreciate it. For a larger chain, take the survey at the bottom of your receipt and praise a specific employee by name (they may get a bonus).

PUT DOWN YOUR PHONE

Fully engage with the person in front of you.

WRITE A LETTER

When your friend receives a handwritten letter from you, they'll admire it like a paleontologist who has just discovered a new dinosaur fossil.

EMPATHIZE

Remember that everyone is dealing with their own personal struggles that you know nothing about.

BE NICE INDISCRIMINATELY

Be as nice to someone working a minimum wage job as to the CEO. Everyone is cut from the same cloth.

BE NICE TO YOURSELF

After you've been nice to others, offer yourself some compassion, too. No one is perfect. You have a nice smile. And you made someone else smile today.

LGBTQ

SEX VS. GENDER

In all likelihood, you know people who identify as LGBTQ, even if you're unaware of it. To give them the love and respect everyone deserves, this section will give you a very basic understanding of what LGBTQ means.

Sex vs. Gender

First, think of sex and gender as two different concepts. **SEX** can refer to someone's biology or anatomy, whereas **GENDER** is their concept of themself, or their gender *identity*.

ALPHABET SOUP

Besides LGBTQ, you may see more letters (or a + symbol) to represent those who aren't accurately represented by LGBTQ alone. For brevity, we'll define just five letters.

L - LESBIAN
refers to a woman who is attracted (emotionally, romantically, and/or physically) to other women.

G - GAY
refers to an individual who is attracted to people of the same sex.

B - BISEXUAL
(or "bi") refers to an individual attracted to both men and women.

T - TRANSGENDER
(or "trans") describes a person's gender identity that does not match their assigned sex at birth.

ALPHABET SOUP

Q - QUEER
is used by some LGBTQ individuals to describe their community, but others dislike the term. **QUESTIONING** describes those who are in a process of discovery and exploration about their sexual orientation or gender identity.

You may also hear the terms **NONBINARY** for individuals whose gender identity is neither exclusively masculine nor feminine, **ASEXUAL** for someone who does not experience sexual attraction, and **PANSEXUAL** for attraction toward people regardless of their sex or gender identity. Many more terms exist, but this list is a start.

PRONOUNS

You may see he/him/his, she/her/hers, or they/them/their in email signatures. Why? Since gender identity is a wide spectrum, they are simply eliminating the guesswork for you.

By now, you're probably familiar with this book's protagonist, Alex, who is nonbinary. We use the pronouns they/them/their for Alex.

STRIVE TO BE AN ALLY AND ADVOCATE OF LGBTQ INDIVIDUALS AND THE LGBTQ COMMUNITY.

HOW TO BE SUPPORTIVE

EDUCATE YOURSELF
Research gender identity and discriminatory policies affecting your friends, family, or anyone. Listen and keep an open mind.

USE YOUR VOICE
Speak up when you see or hear others making hurtful comments or LGBTQ jokes. Vote for politicians who pledge to enact policies that will keep the LGBTQ community safe.

BE RESPECTFUL
Do not out someone as part of the LGBTQ community, since you could jeopardize their safety. Do not ask someone about their genitalia (this sounds incredibly obvious, but it's necessary to include). Do not use someone's previous name (e.g., Paul) if they've transitioned to a new name (e.g., Paula).

HEALTH

PHYSICAL HEALTH

EXERCISE

Aim for 25 minutes (26 if training for a marathon) of exercise three or more times per week. Think of it as a *Walking Dead* episode on exercising where you're the main star.

To keep it fun, switch up your workout medium. Use a gym, YouTube workouts, or even a local sports recreation league. Do strength-training exercises for all major muscle groups at least twice a week.

In terms of workout intensity, remember this simple rule: the less intense the exercise, the more time it'll take to get the same effect.

REDUCE SITTING

Prolonged sitting has been shown to raise the risk of type 2 diabetes, heart disease, and premature death. Every 20–30 minutes, get up and stand or take a short walk.

DRINK PLENTY OF WATER

While your weight and activity level will vary, the typical recommendation is to drink two liters of water per day. Plus lots of water will force you to reduce sitting when you walk to the bathroom.

FOOD

Keep it fresh and colorful. Get at least five servings of fruits and veggies per day. Give your body

PHYSICAL HEALTH

proteins and carbs, and electrolytes after working out. And remember, pasta never goes out of style, even if it's multigrain.

GET ENOUGH SLEEP

Get 7–8 hours of sleep a night. Poor sleeping habits are linked to seemingly endless health concerns, including funny marks around your eyes.

TAKE CARE OF YOUR TEETH

You kept every baby tooth you ever lost. So keep your adult teeth as well: brush twice a day and always floss.

MENTAL HEALTH

STAY CONNECTED WITH OLD FRIENDS

Along with self-driving cars and *Stranger Things*, the 21st century has also brought us cell phones. Call your family and friends. They miss you more than you know.

FIND COMMUNITY WITH NEW FRIENDS

Community can be found everywhere. Search out what you love, whether it's sports, art, or church, and like-minded people will come your way.

DON'T FORGET TO CRY

For some reason, salt water dripping from our eyes makes the world seem a whole lot clearer. Crying is natural and cathartic. So, whenever needed, let those healing waters flow.

IDENTITY THEFT

TIPS TO PROTECT YOURSELF

You can't actually steal someone's identity. You know all those Elvis impersonators? Not actually Elvis. We're pretty sure they're not using his credit card, either.

Identity theft typically means using someone's personal information to steal money. Not only may victims lose money, but also their credit histories can be damaged.

College students and young graduates are highly vulnerable because of their high use of technology (file sharing, social networking sites, etc.), the avalanche of credit card offers they throw in the trash, the wide use of Social Security numbers for identification, and how infrequently they review their credit card and checking accounts. So what can you do?

GUARD YOUR INFORMATION

Tear up all of your credit card statements and offers, ATM and gas receipts, and other personal documents. Keep your computer and wireless network password-protected. Remember that others can hear you when you yell into your cell phone in a crowded place. Avoid logging into your online bank or credit card accounts while using public Wi-Fi. Pay particular attention to protecting your Social Security number, which can open the door for bad guys to apply for credit in your good name. Don't keep your Social Security card in your wallet.

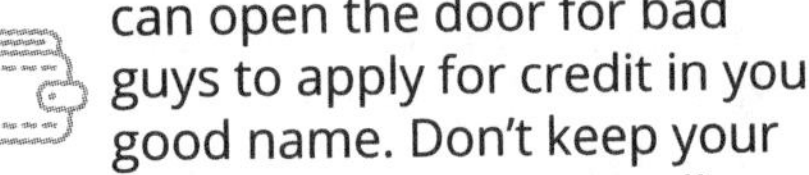

TIPS TO PROTECT YOURSELF

If a company with which you have an account notifies you of a data breach, change your password.

Even if you're a computer whiz, you can get burned in low-tech ways. **DUMPSTER DIVING** (going through the trash), **SHOULDER SURFING** (criminals sneaking a peek at your credit card), and **SKIMMING** (restaurant servers selling your credit card numbers) are common.

MONITOR

The three credit bureaus are required by law to provide you with a free credit report every year (see AnnualCreditReport.com). Learn more about credit reports in our **CREDIT** topic in the **MONEY** section. Also, review your credit card and checking account statements carefully each month.

PROBLEMS

If something goes wrong (e.g., your credit card number is stolen), request that a "fraud alert" be placed on your file with the three major credit bureaus (Experian, TransUnion, and Equifax). Tell them that you're an identity theft victim, and be vigilant in clearing your name. Report the identity theft to the Federal Trade Commission at identitytheft.gov.

MORTALITY

OVERVIEW

Don't you hate it when someone tells you how a movie will end? Spoiler alert: one day, you're going to die.

"No way!" you say. Well, we reviewed the statistics, and they're convincing.

Since the authors of this topic are (currently) alive, we don't actually know what happens when you die. But millions of people have clinically died (their hearts and breathing have stopped) but were resuscitated, and many have described their near-death experiences.

Are these stories for real? Who knows, but the experience is surprisingly consistent across cultures, continents, and age groups:

- an awareness of being dead
- an out-of-body experience (floating while watching doctors work on their bodies)
- movement toward a powerful light (sometimes through a tunnel)
- intense feelings of peace and unconditional love

- a fleeting view of their entire life histories (beyond Facebook)
- a sensation of sharing experiences with every person they have known.

To learn more, search the web for "near-death experiences."

FUNERALS

If you don't enjoy reading about topics related to mortality, we ask you to imagine five fluffy kittens to lift your spirits.

Not working? Try *ten* kittens! Go ahead, imagine them.

Now, watch those kittens play. Oh my goodness, one just fell over. Isn't he cute?

FUNERAL COSTS

Funerals can be crazy expensive, but you have a number of affordable options.

PYRAMID BURIAL

(under $5 billion) Hire 30,000 laborers over twenty years to build a 400-foot-tall pyramid with limestone blocks.

TRADITIONAL PLUS BURIAL

(up to $10,000) The traditional funeral involves embalming (preserving the body for viewing), viewing of the body, a formal funeral service, transportation by hearse to the cemetery, and burial.

DIRECT BURIAL

(often under $4,000) The body is buried shortly after death within a simple container. Since there is no viewing, embalming is unnecessary.

CREMATION

(often under $4,000) Burning the body before or after a funeral service creates remains that can be stored in an urn, scattered at sea, or even made into works of art or jewelry.

DONATING TO SCIENCE

(often free) Donate your body to a medical school for teaching and research (search for "anatomical gift program").

Imagine those kittens again. Oh dear, did two of them just kiss when they bopped noses?

That's so precious.

FUNERAL OBLIGATIONS

If a family member dies, you may be surprised to discover that you've been named the "executor" of his or her estate. The what?

As the **EXECUTOR**, you'll handle the property, pay debts and taxes, and distribute what's left to those who are entitled to it. Even if you feel an obligation, you can decline this role, and the job will pass to someone else.

If you accept these duties, rely on the help of others to lessen your work. Where do you start?

DECEASED

Your family member may have a will and/or a living will. Locate these documents for funeral and burial instructions, if any.

FUNERAL DIRECTOR

This professional is paid to handle many of the duties you'd never considered (e.g., paperwork).

PROFESSIONALS

If your loved one had an accountant, attorney, or insurance agent, contact him or her for help and direction regarding the will, money, etc.

LIFE INSURANCE

"Wait, now we're talking about *my* death?" you might be thinking. Again, it's possible that you might die one day.

But for the sake of holding your interest, this topic is actually to share with your *friends* who don't have this book. Here are some things that *they* should know.

How does it work? A **BENEFICIARY** (the person named in the life insurance policy) receives money (the **FACE AMOUNT**) when your friend dies.

Who needs it? If you're a new graduate without a spouse or kids, it's really optional. But once you get married, then game on. Note that life insurance is less expensive when you're younger.

LIFE INSURANCE TYPES

TERM LIFE

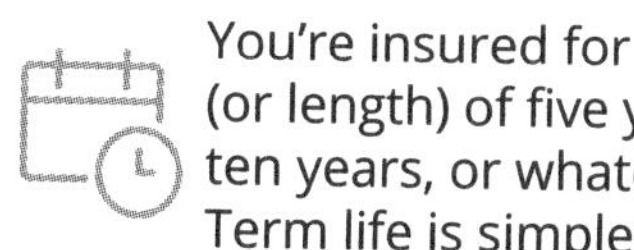

You're insured for a term (or length) of five years, ten years, or whatever. Term life is simple: if you die, it makes a payment to your beneficiary. If you stop paying your monthly premiums or if your term ends, you're no longer covered.

WHOLE LIFE

You're insured for your whole life—it's "permanent" life insurance. This type of life insurance not only pays money when you die, but also includes something similar to a savings account in it. For this reason, whole life is usually more expensive than term life. As a new graduate, consider getting term life for its lower cost and simplicity.

GETTING LIFE INSURANCE

You can get life insurance a few different ways.

EMPLOYER INSURANCE

You may discover that you already have life insurance through your employer, but it's usually a fairly small policy (two to three times your salary).

GET YOUR OWN POLICY

If you get your own policy, you'll probably be able to get a larger face amount than what you can get at your job.

Getting a policy *when you're healthy* usually protects your right to maintain life insurance, even when you're sick. If you wait and get a policy when you're on your deathbed, you'll probably be out of luck.

Look for life insurance through an agent or your alumni association. Whatever you do, shop around for the best price and the best insurance company.

INTERNATIONAL TRAVEL

TIPS AND TRICKS

Traveling to a new country may be "sick," but not when you're *sick*. Or jet-lagged, under-organized, or unsafe. Here are a few tips on how to safeguard that international trip of a lifetime.

CONSIDER TIME ZONES

When booking connecting flights, keep in mind that international flights may depart on one day and arrive on the next. It might feel like time travel, but planes don't use flux capacitors.

CHECK YOUR CREDIT CARDS

Prior to your departure, contact your credit card or debit card to alert the company that you'll be making foreign transactions. Otherwise, your card may get rejected—hurting its self-esteem—thus making the transactions appear fraudulent. Consider getting a card without a foreign transaction fee (or learn how much you'll pay on your current card).

PACK WISELY

Pack a change of clothes in your carry-on. If your luggage gets lost, at least you can feel clean and refreshed while you hit up the local clothing stores for your brand new style.

Pack a charger adapter. The outlets in other countries likely won't be compatible with your electronics.

TIPS AND TRICKS

PLAN FOR YOUR PHONE CALLS

The international plan from your current provider might be the easiest but most expensive option. Look into inexpensive prepaid phones or SIM cards that you can insert into your existing phone. Sadly, carrier pigeons don't operate internationally. The ocean's just too darn big.

PRINT OUT YOUR PAPERS

Make copies of your passport, visa, credit cards, prescriptions, and itinerary (such as plane and hotel details) and keep copies in your carry-on and with a family member.

CHECK YOUR PASSPORT

Even if your passport is still current, some countries won't let you in if your passport is set to expire in the next *six months*.

PREP FOR TAXIS

Once you arrive, bring a brochure or business card from your hotel when you go out on the town. On the return home, it can save you from a confusing, four-hour taxi ride if your driver doesn't speak the same language or if your bad pronunciation just sounds like gargling to the locals.

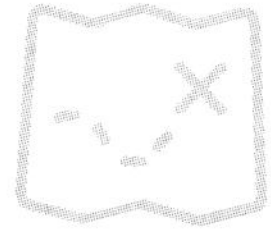

CARRY LOCAL CURRENCY

Don't convert your money at the airport conversion centers; it may seem convenient, but they'll rip you off. Instead, go to a bank or ATM when you arrive at your destination. Find out what fees your bank charges for international ATM withdrawals.

STAY HEALTHY

In countries where water can make you sick, remember that water doesn't always come in a glass. Avoid ice and salad. (Vegetables are often washed in tap water.) Stick with boiled or fully cooked food. Brush your teeth with bottled water and keep your eyes and mouth closed in the shower.

TIPS AND TRICKS

LEARN SOME OF THE LANGUAGE

"Thank you," "please," "excuse me," and "sorry" are always good. "Ugh, you eat this?" is bad.

BE THOUGHTFUL WITH YOUR CAMERA

While parts of your trip might look great in a frame, an anonymous building or child may be someone else's home or son. Don't be afraid to ask if it's OK to take a photo.

DRESS RESPECTFULLY

Just because you dress a certain way in your daily life doesn't mean that it's acceptable in other countries. Research ahead of time to know what's decent and respectful.

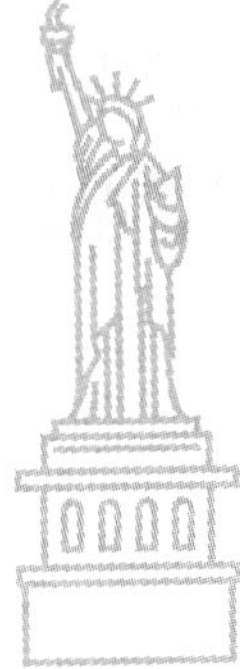

TRAVEL INSURANCE

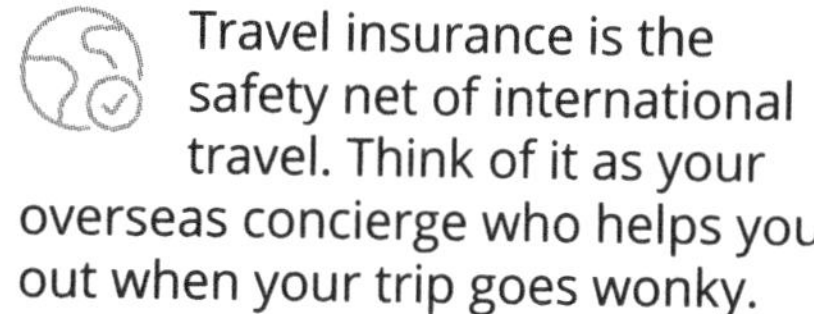

Travel insurance is the safety net of international travel. Think of it as your overseas concierge who helps you out when your trip goes wonky.

Check with your health insurance provider and credit card, but in most cases, you probably won't have much insurance coverage when you leave the country. You'll want to consider two types of travel insurance.

MEDICAL POLICIES

Since your regular health insurance may not cover all of your medical expenses when you take your annual "running of the bulls" vacation in Spain, these plans fill in the gaps and typically provide 1) emergency medical and dental treatment and 2) medical evacuation coverage, in case you have to return to the US in a hurry (say, with a bull-horn-shaped hole in your abdomen).

PACKAGE POLICIES

These plans "package" medical expenses and many other things that might go wrong. When people refer to generic "travel insurance," they're often referring to a package policy. Some of the extra coverage often includes:

- trip cancellation (some conditions may apply)
- missed connections
- lost, stolen, damaged, or delayed baggage
- travel delays (due to weather, accident, Godzilla, etc.).

Some package plans also cover incidents like rental car accidents, identity theft, damage to sports equipment (in case your golf clubs "somehow" end up in the pond during your 100-stroke round), and adventure travel coverage.

Package plans often cost between 5% and 8% of the cost of the trip, depending on how much coverage you buy. Medical plans are less expensive.

So, should you purchase travel insurance? It all depends on what you're willing to risk. If you feel OK paying for random crises, then save yourself the money and have a great trip.

VOTE

A BIG WHOOP

All around the world, voting is a pretty big whoop. Some people are pretty serious about voting. Other people are really serious and courageous.

In 1993, rebel guerrillas in Peru dynamited two buses on the day of elections to prevent people from voting. So people walked.

In 2004, Taliban insurgents distributed pamphlets threatening women with execution if they took part in Afghanistan's elections. And women still voted.

We could fill the rest of this book with examples, but if people risk their lives to vote and if women and African Americans spent decades in this country fighting for the right to vote, it's probably a whoop. In fact, it's probably a really big whoop.

But it's not just an abstract whoop. Your vote affects you on a very *personal* level. You elect people who affect your take-home pay, personal safety, streets, privacy, medical care, student loan rates, job prospects, and the air you breathe. You should also care about the other people affected by your vote. Here's the scoop.

REGISTER

To become an official voter, you need to register. It's usually as simple as filling out a one-page form, but the process varies a little from state to state (visit Vote411.org). At the very least, you'll need to provide proof of residence in the district where you're registering, such as mail delivered to you or a signed lease listing your current address.

POLITICAL PARTIES

When you register, you're typically asked to join a **POLITICAL PARTY**. Think of each party as a "team" first and a set of beliefs second. Although parties have some basic ideologies, the web of issues and policies can vary with candidates and elections over time. Many voters do not identify with everything in a specific party platform.

OFFICIAL BALLOT

REPUBLICANS	DEMOCRATS	ADDITIONAL PARTIES
☐ They're often represented by their red color (on political maps), the term GOP (Grand Old Party), and their elephant logo. Relative to Democrats, Republicans generally believe in lower taxes, less government (wanting citizens to make more of their own decisions), and social conservative issues.	☐ They're often represented by their blue color on political maps and their donkey logo. Relative to Republicans, Democrats generally believe in progressive taxes (higher taxes for higher earners), more of a government role in citizens' lives (stricter gun control and more regulation on businesses), and liberal social issues (protecting the environment).	☐ **THE LIBERTARIAN PARTY** favors few restrictions on businesses and strong civil liberties (freedom of speech). They are not to be confused with the **LIBRARIAN PARTY**, which favors order and silence. ☐ **THE GREEN PARTY** advocates environmentalism and nonviolence. ☐ **INDEPENDENTS** may not be able to particpate in **PRIMARIES** (elections within a party).

VOTING PLACE

Use Vote411.org to find your polling place (usually only minutes from your home and quick), but if you live in on-campus housing, you may need to get an **ABSENTEE BALLOT** (also found on Vote411.org) sent to your home state if you are registered there.

READ

Many politicians court the ignorant vote. Don't be part of this prized demographic. News and candidates' websites contain a wealth of good voting information.

VOTE

On Election Day, the "I Voted" sticker becomes the must-have fashion accessory.

Everyone has one. The red and blue goes with almost any outfit, and it gives the "I'm responsible" vibe to friends. You'll not only get this sticker, but deep inside your heart, you'll know that you're a very big whoop.

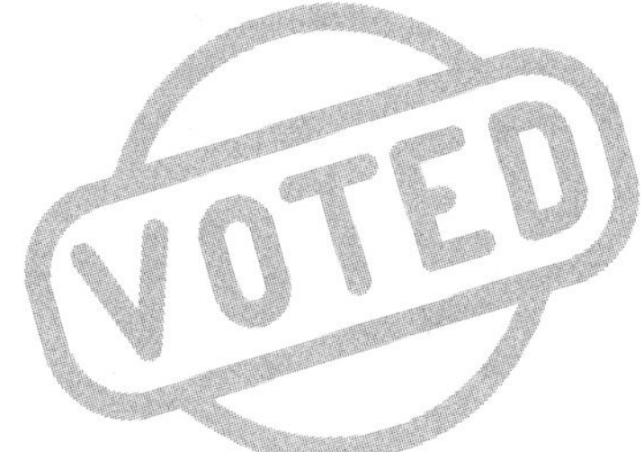

WATCHING FOOTBALL

PREP

If you already watch *SportsCenter*, then this topic isn't for you. But if football doesn't interest you, how can you enjoy watching the "big game" with friends?

PICK A TEAM

When you have someone to root for, the game is a lot more fun. Search Google for a story about a player. Or just pick the team with the colors or mascot you like.

MAKE A BET

You don't have to risk money, but if you wager a face full of peanut butter, then the game gets a lot more interesting.

THE RULES

The game is divided into four 15-minute quarters. But expect it to take a lot longer than 60 minutes—because the clock stops for lots of reasons.

One team (say, the "Antelopes") starts on **OFFENSE**. They get to hold the ball and, they hope, score points.

The other team (say, the "Cheetahs") starts on **DEFENSE**. They try to stop the Antelopes from scoring points.

The Antelopes want to reach the other end of the field with the ball. But the Cheetahs want to eat—er, tackle the Antelopes to prevent them from scoring.

THE RULES

Note: Any player who eats another player on the field potentially faces a multi-game suspension.

Players on each team line up with their butts in the air along an imaginary line. When the Antelopes say go, the Cheetahs attack.

The Antelopes are, like, "Aaaa! Where's my mother? And why is this guy from *National Geographic* taking pictures of me?"

The Antelopes either **RUN** the ball (literally hold the ball and run with it) or **PASS** the ball (when the handsome **QUARTERBACK** throws the ball to a teammate).

Once the Cheetahs tackle the player with the ball, the **PLAY** is stopped, and everyone lines up again.

SCORING

If a player reaches the end of the field (the **END ZONE**) while holding the ball, he scores a **TOUCHDOWN** (worth 6 points, with a chance to earn 1 or 2 more). At this point, you should get really excited or crazy angry.

If a team gets close to the end zone but doesn't reach it, it can kick the ball between two posts for a **FIELD GOAL** (3 points).

DOWNS

If a team stayed in one place play after play and never made progress, then the game would be really boring to everyone, not just to you.

To keep the game interesting, your friends pay attention to "downs." As a team tries to score, it has to keep making progress down the field. Otherwise it loses the ball. When you hear stuff like **1ST AND 10**, this means:

1ST = THE DOWN

Think of each down (the 1st, 2nd, 3rd, or 4th) as a chance for a team to advance down the field.

10 = YARDS

That is, the number of yards remaining to prove a team's progress.

DOWNS

Here's the important part: if a team moves the ball at least 10 yards after 4 downs, it earns a new 1st down.

"What? This sounds like calculus!" you say. But keep reading, and soon your friends will call you "Football Einstein."

A team always starts at 1st and 10. Now bust out your pen and paper:

PLAY #1:

The Antelopes run for 3 yards, so now it's "2nd and 7" (7 because they started with 10 yards, and you subtract the 3 yards they ran).

PLAY #2:

They pass for 8 yards, so they earned a new 1st and 10 (because they needed only 7 yards and got 8, so they showed adequate progress). Hooray!

With their progress, they're farther down the field (closer to scoring points) and rewarded with more plays (downs 1, 2, 3, and 4). But if they fail to show progress, if they fail to go 10 yards in 4 downs, they'll have to give the ball to the Cheetahs.

ALUMNI GIVING

VALUE

If you're just coming out of school, giving money back to your alma mater, fraternity, or sorority is probably the last thing on your mind. Actually, if you thought of the last thing on your mind, alumni giving might be just behind that.

Schools know that you're starting a new job or entering graduate school, buying a car, paying loans, or—to put things more succinctly—broke. Why, then, do they bother you, a new graduate, for a $10 or $25 donation?

They want your **PARTICIPATION**, even if it's small. Why?

RANKINGS

For better or for worse, many people judge the stature of a school based on the college rankings in *US News & World Report*.

Five percent of a school's overall ranking in *US News* is based on "alumni satisfaction,"

which is based on only one factor: **percentage of alumni giving**. Since the giving rate is usually lowest among young alumni, increased participation can have a real impact on rankings.

FUNDING

Many colleges apply for grants from foundations that require a school to include its alumni-giving participation in its application. More alumni-giving participation can result in more grants for the school.

Participation not only helps the school but also helps you as well. For the rest of your life, you're branded (on a place on your back that you can see only with two mirrors) as "a graduate of XYZ school." Every time you apply for a job or your team wins a game, you're an XYZ graduate to your friends and colleagues. A more "prestigious" school can increase the value of your degree.

MONEY ADDS UP

Even if your giving is small, you'd be surprised at how quickly gifts in the $10 to $100 range add up. Giving helps bridge the gap between tuition received and the cost of running a school, which can be huge when you factor in financial aid, salaries, building maintenance, and so on.

OMMM

MEDITATION

Imagine hearing of a miracle drug that improves memory, attention, positive emotions, energy, and your immune system. Now imagine that this same drug lowers anxiety, stress, high blood pressure, and depression. Now imagine that this drug were free and easily available.

Would you be spending a lot of time imagining things? Yes. Would you also ask, "What is this miracle drug?" If you read the title of this page, you know that it's meditation. If you didn't read the title of this page, then it's meditation.

To oversimplify, meditation is taking time out of your day to clear your mind. To start, you might close your eyes and try to focus just on your breathing. As thoughts enter your mind, try to "return to your breath."

So let's try now. Commit the text in the diagram below to memory and close your eyes.

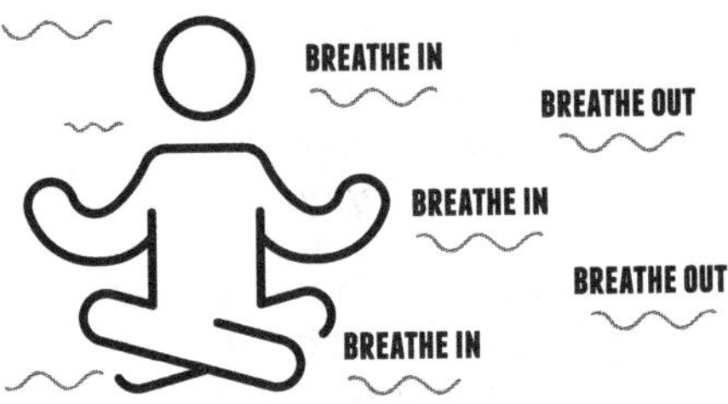

If you're thinking about something other than your breath (you know you are), just watch these thoughts float by and focus on your breath again.

That's it. Try this for 5–10 minutes every day. You might love it. At a minimum, you'll have something to talk about with your friends.

SECTION THREE:

AUTO

It took four hours for the dealer to realize that Lisa Carr was her *name*, not her *purpose*.

BUYING VS. LEASING A CAR

OVERVIEW

Basically, the better choice between buying and leasing a car depends on the individual.

If you want a new car every three years, a lease might be best for you. A lease is simple, with minimal unknown costs. If you want to keep a car for a while, buying will save you money in the long run.

Before we start, you need to master the leasing jargon.

JARGON

RESIDUAL VALUE

Value of your car at the end of the lease.

CAPITALIZED COST

Amount you borrow.

"CAN'T GO LOWER"

Lies. All lies.

LEASING PROS AND CONS

(+) LEASES USUALLY HAVE LOWER MONTHLY PAYMENTS

When you lease, you aren't paying for the whole car. Instead, you're paying for the difference in the car's value now versus its value at the end of the lease, plus interest and fees.

(+) LEASES HAVE NO REPAIR COSTS

Since your car is new, it will be under warranty over the life of the lease. If you own a car, your warranty will eventually end.

(+) LATEST AND GREATEST

If the latest automobile technology gets you excited, leasing allows you to drive a brand new car every few years. A CD player (or cassette player) might not be super useful over time.

(-) LEASES HAVE HIGHER INSURANCE PREMIUMS

Since you don't own the car, the leasing company gets to call the shots when it comes to insurance. They usually require more than minimum state standards. Remember to factor in this cost when comparing choices.

(-) LEASES HAVE RESTRICTIONS

A lease charges you extra fees for driving too many miles. When you own, you can drive as much as you want.

(-) LEASE PAYMENTS NEVER END

If you lease a car and then lease again, your payments never end. When you buy a car, you'll eventually pay it off.

(-) TERMINATION COSTS

Terminating your lease early can be very expensive. If you own a car, you can sell it at any point.

AUTO INSURANCE

BASIC TYPES

Everyone needs auto insurance. Here's the gist.

BODILY INJURY LIABILITY

Pays for injuries you cause to *someone else*. This insurance is required in most states.

PROPERTY DAMAGE LIABILITY

Pays for damages to someone else's car, mailbox, garage, or pool (another story for another day). This is required in most states.

PERSONAL INJURY PROTECTION (PIP)

Pays for injuries to the driver and passengers of your car. This is required in some states.

COLLISION

Pays for your car when you get in a wreck. If you own a clunker, don't waste your money with this coverage. You'll end up spending more money in coverage than the value of any damages.

COMPREHENSIVE

Pays for damage to your car due to theft, earthquake, raining frogs (name the movie), or other things not wreck-related.

UNINSURED (OR UNDERINSURED) MOTORIST

Pays for your injuries when you get into an accident with an uninsured (or underinsured) motorist.

THAT "20/40/10" THING

Most insurance policies and state standards are written in a funny code with slash marks. This will help you translate.

FIRST NUMBER (20)

Your insurance carrier pays a maximum of $20,000 in medical bills (bodily injury liability) for *one person per accident*.

SECOND NUMBER (40)

Your carrier pays a maximum of $40,000 in medical bills for *all people per accident* (total). So if three people are injured in an accident, your insurance company could pay up to $40,000, but not more.

THIRD NUMBER (10)

Your insurance carrier pays a maximum of $10,000 for all *property damage* (e.g., you drive into a building) per accident.

NO-FAULT

Some states have a thing called a no-fault law. This means that your insurance carrier covers your bodily injury and property damage no matter who caused the accident.

BUYING TIPS

ASK ABOUT DISCOUNTS

You might benefit if you drive below a certain number of miles per year and have anti-theft devices.

COMBINE POLICIES

You may get a discount if you buy both auto and renter's insurance (for your apartment) through the same company.

SHOP AROUND

Insurance premiums vary greatly.

DRIVE SAFELY

You'll pay less for insurance when you're not a terror on wheels.

AUTO CARE

OVERVIEW

Cars are like the mechanical version of Benjamin Button. They start off wise beyond their years, but after they age a bit, they need a little help from their parents. As the legal guardian of your vehicle, use these tips to keep your "kid" happy and healthy.

STAY LEGIT

Every year or two, you'll need to renew your auto **REGISTRATION** (look for a letter in the mail). To renew, you may need an **INSPECTION** from a local mechanic and proof of **INSURANCE** to prove you're safe to drive.

Once you renew, many states will send you a cute little sticker for your license plate or window and a paper for your glove compartment or wallet. Then if you ever get pulled over and asked for your license and registration, you can say, "Hey, I have that!"

GENERAL MAINTENANCE

OIL CHANGES

Some people recommend changing your oil every 3,000 miles, but for most cars between 5,000 and 7,500 miles should be fine. Check your owner's manual. If your car's really granola, it might even ask for olive oil.

TIRE PRESSURE

For increased safety and gas mileage, keep your tires properly inflated. To check, buy a **TIRE PRESSURE GAUGE** (or watch for a warning on your dashboard). The recommended pressure can be found on the sticker inside your driver's side door. Inflate your tires at a gas station for a buck or two. If you have a leak, a tire mechanic may be able to add a **PATCH** instead of selling you a new tire.

WINTER/SUMMER TIRES

If you live in a place where it snows a lot, get **SNOW TIRES** (instead of all-season tires) for the winter season.

BATTERIES

Surprise! Most cars won't give you a low-battery warning, but rather will just give you the silent treatment in the middle of the Target parking lot. An average battery lasts only about three years.

Roadside assistance. When your car doesn't start, have a backup plan (a.k.a. an auto service) to drive to you and replace your battery. You may already have **ROADSIDE ASSISTANCE** from your credit card, cell phone plan, car warranty, or auto insurance (check now). If you don't, lots of options exist online.

Self-help. Alternatively, you can buy **JUMPER CABLES** or a **PORTABLE CHARGER** to get your car started long enough to drive to a mechanic.

AUTO ACCIDENTS

OVERVIEW

You've watched every *Fast and Furious* movie six times, so you think you know what to do when your bumper is hanging from your car. But here's a little secret: *some parts of this epic franchise aren't realistic*. If you're not Vin Diesel, these tips will help.

STOP

If you get into an accident, don't leave the scene, even if it's minor. If you leave, you'll be committing a hit-and-run, which will get you in a lot of trouble with the law.

KEEP YOUR CAR SAFE

If possible, pull over to the side of the road. If you can't, put on your hazard lights. If you're on a freeway, be extra careful, since cars going 80 mph don't play games. Vin Diesel might jump off a bridge at this point, but you should stay put.

OVERVIEW

KEEP ALL HUMANS SAFE

If another driver is involved, check on them and call for medical assistance if necessary. If you're both OK, meet on the shoulder, as far from traffic as possible.

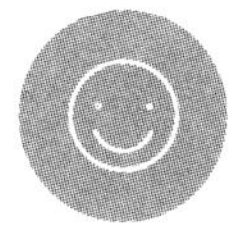

BE KIND

Even though your first instinct may be to blow a gasket, try to extinguish it. Be calm and offer up a smile. You've both just joined the club called "I Had a Bad Day."

CALL THE POLICE

In many states, you legally have to call the police, even if the accident is minor. The police may decline to respond if your accident is minor and no one is hurt, but you should let them decide. You may also need a police report to file an insurance claim.

GATHER INFORMATION

Exchange driver's license numbers, names, phone numbers, and insurance information; take photos of any damage; and notify your insurance company right away. Witnesses are key, so note if anybody was there when it all went down.

SECTION FOUR:

HOME

Jenny proved too immature to be a Realtor.

GETTING YOUR APARTMENT

OVERVIEW

As you probably expect, getting an apartment varies tremendously from city to city.

In this section, we'll explain some universal truths that you'll need to know for apartment shopping in virtually any city.

As Alex's senior year was winding down, they took the role of a "casual observer" in their preparation for the apartment hunt. In other words, Alex didn't do anything.

Alex planned on staying on a friend's couch for a few days, casually checking apartment listings, and finding an ad that read:

HUGE ONE-BEDROOM. $100/MO. RENTING ONLY TO PEOPLE NAMED ALEX.

Six months and three couches later, Alex finally found a place to call home.

This topic will help you avoid some of Alex's pitfalls. Not only will it help you find an apartment, but it will help you find a place that you'll like for the next few years. Anyone can find an overpriced, tiny apartment in a run-down area of town. We'll help you find a place you can be proud to call your own.

BEFORE YOU GET THERE

Set alerts on apartment websites. Be the first to know when new listings show up with your specifications.

DON'T RULE OUT OPTIONS TOO EARLY

Some websites let you filter apartments by pool, social spaces,

etc. After you see a place, you may be surprised by what you like and don't like. Spend time visiting places before you rule them out.

BE CAUTIOUS OF SCAMS

If a listing sounds too good to be true, it usually is. No one rents a six-bedroom apartment with a pool for $200 a month.

BE PROFESSIONAL

If you reach out to a landlord for a viewing, sound professional, polite, and reliable. Don't say, "Your apartment isn't as bad as some of the others I've seen. I don't have much money, but I'm quiet between 1:00 and 3:00 a.m." You may hear that your apartment "was just taken."

SPREAD THE WORD

One of the most important things you can do prior to your move is to tell people that you're looking for an apartment.

Tell anyone and everyone you know. You'd be amazed at how many apartments never make it onto the rental market.

You'll never know if your best friend's sister's boyfriend's brother's girlfriend heard from this guy who knows this kid who's going with a girl...who might be renting out an apartment next month.

Tell everyone. You never know.

ROOMMATES

You may be looking forward to finally living on your own, but a roommate can significantly cut the price you pay in rent.

Why? The bathroom and the kitchen are the most expensive rooms in an apartment. The fixtures, appliances, and plumbing are expensive for your landlord to buy and maintain. When you have a roommate, you're essentially splitting these costs.

Also, don't underestimate the value of a roommate for security and social reasons, especially if you're moving to a city.

CREDIT ISSUES

When you finally find an apartment, your landlord will check your credit before giving you the keys.

Believe it or not, every single credit card bill and loan payment you ever made is recorded by a credit agency. Your landlord will check to see if you pay your bills. If you have bad credit, you'll have the adult equivalent of cooties.

Learn more in the **CREDIT** topic of this book.

UP-FRONT PAYMENTS

Once you've got your credit in order, start saving some money.

Depending on what city you'll be moving to, you may need a lot of money up front to get a place.

Most new apartments require at least one month's rent up front. Others can require the first month, the last month, a security deposit (the equivalent of a month), and a broker's fee. This works out to: four months' rent up front.

Four months is the rare exception, but most book writers like to include the most extreme cases to make the text more dramatic!!

UP-FRONT PAYMENTS

We called home after we got our first apartments and talked to our folks. "The good news is I got a place. The bad news is I spent all my cash. I'm broke and hungry." Parents love phone calls like that.

When you go to sign your lease, your landlord likely won't accept an out-of-state check for your deposit. He or she will require a **CASH EQUIVALENT**, like a money order or a cashier's check.

These two items are considered "cash equivalents" because they can't bounce. You need to have money in your account for your bank to issue you a cash equivalent. The bank will hold this money in your account until your money order or cashier's check clears.

When the time comes to pay for your apartment, you could arrive with a briefcase full of twenties in the trunk of your Subaru (plus a crowbar, in case you need to "persuade" the superintendent to keep the rent fair).

Alternately, set up an account in a bank that has a branch in your new city. Then you can get a cashier's check. Set up your account early: your bank may require a week's wait before you can write checks.

If possible, sign up for automatic payments by check or credit card. You may get a discount and you won't forget to pay (saving you late fees).

APARTMENT LINGO

Here is some of the lingo you may see in apartment ads.

WALK-UP
No elevator

DUPLEX
Two-unit building

ALCOVE
Partly enclosed area connected to a room

STUDIO
One room or one room connected to a kitchen

JUNIOR ONE-BEDROOM
Tiny room off the living room, which may fit only a bed

WASHER/DRYER HOOKUPS
Machines not included, but you can buy and install your own

ABBREV.

As you're looking at ads, you'll quickly be amazed at the liberties taken with the English language. You may confuse many of the ads with a word scramble puzzle. These are some common abbreviations:

H/W
Hardwood floors

DW
Dishwasher

EIK
Eat-in kitchen (eat where the food is made)

WIC
Walk-in closet

W/D
Washer and dryer

BROKERS

In some cities, you'll have to use a broker. In other spots, they don't even exist. Brokers basically own the market in some large cities.

At the same time, brokers can serve as a great resource. They may turn out to be your best friend... because brokers' hearts are just so darn big—or because they get paid handsome commissions when they find you an apartment.

Always lowball your price. If you can pay only $800, tell the broker you can pay only $600.

No matter what kind of apartment you need, you're going to hear the same thing: "Wow, I don't have a lot of listings in that price range, but I do have apartments for $200 more." You'll say, "That's convenient, because I was hoping not to have any money for food and silly little things like that."

Think of this as a game of poker. If you show your broker your cards right away, they're going to raise you until you're broke. (Or brok-er. Get it? Get it?)

Do not put your full faith in one broker. Use many. You're going to pay one a lot of money. Make them work a little bit for your cash.

Don't feel bad saying no 100 times. They're used to it.

THINGS TO CHECK

When you're looking at places, make a list of things to check. Once you move in, you'll enjoy those trivial extras like running water and a toilet that flushes. Remember to check:

- light switches
- elevator
- air conditioner
- heat
- appliances
- noise level
- hot water
- windows
- leaks under sink
- damages
- proximity to subway
- parking

Also check utilities. What do you have to pay? Depending on your weather, your heat or AC may be expensive in different seasons. If you don't pay for heat, you might be able to afford a more expensive place.

After you've looked at the place with a broker, pull this sneaky little trick.

TELL YOUR BROKER THAT YOU FORGOT YOUR COAT (PURSE, DENTURES, WHATEVER) IN THE APARTMENT. GO BACK "TO GET IT" WHILE YOUR BROKER WAITS FOR YOU OUTSIDE.

Once you return to the apartment, ask the current tenant or a neighbor a few questions. You'll get unbiased, honest answers. Is the apartment loud? Does the super (superintendent) own a wrench?

It might be best to keep looking if you hear, "I don't mind the bugs—they usually keep to themselves."

If you have time, walk around the neighborhood and make sure you feel safe. Try to visit the neighborhood in the day and at night. The night crowd is often dramatically different from the day crowd.

THINGS TO BRING

In many big cities, you'll need to act quickly once you've found your place. In some competitive cities, if you see a place you like, you take it on the spot. There's nothing worse than finding a place you really like, only to have it ripped away by someone who moved faster than you did.

Make sure you have:

- money orders/cash equivalents
- driver's license
- references (from past employers, landlords)
- credit report (you may save money on your rental application if you get the report yourself).

SAMPLE REFERENCE LETTER

If you had a previous landlord, share this template with them:

Dear ___________,

It is with pleasure that I write this letter of recommendation for [name]. When [name] vacated his/her apartment unit, it was in better condition than when he/she moved into it.

During his/her [number]-year residency at [Happy Apartments], [name] was an excellent member of our rental community.

Whenever it snowed, he/she made hot cocoa for all the children and purchased groceries for our older residents.

I will surely miss the smell of [name]'s apple pies filling the hallways and the way he/she sang with the robin on sunny mornings.

I am not a spiritual person by nature, but I do believe that if angels live among us, [name] surely walks among them.

Sincerely,

Property Manager
[Happy Apartments]

SIGNING THE LEASE

The problem with leases is that they are large documents written in small print using big words. The authors try to discourage people from actually reading them.

Take this excerpt from a lease:

ENTIRE AGREEMENT

This agreement contains the entire agreement between parties hereto and neither party is bound by any representations or agreements of any kind except as contained herein.

TRANSLATION

This is your lease.

That being said, make sure you read your lease. These are the things to look for:

- ☑ Make sure the length of the lease is expressly written in the contract. Do not accept a month-to-month contract, or you could get booted.

- ☑ Determine who is responsible for fixing appliances. Some landlords are responsible only for repairing permanent fixtures, such as the sink, shower, and toilet.

- ☑ Confirm that your apartment will be cleaned (and assessed for damage) prior to your arrival. Take photos of all damage and share them with your landlord: “FYI, I can see my neighbor through this giant hole in the floor.”

- ☑ Confirm that your security deposit is going into an interest-bearing account. Most state laws mandate this.

- ☑ Determine your future rent increases. Some states have rent control laws. You never want to be surprised by a massive rent hike once you have all of your stuff on the walls and don’t feel like moving.

- ☑ Make sure your privacy rights are spelled out. Most states require landlords to provide advance notice (usually 24 hours) when they are going to enter your apartment (unless it’s an emergency).

- ☑ Finally, and most important, make sure you have everything in writing. You don’t want to get involved in an argument when your landlord doubles your rent. If everything is in writing, you’ll have a case.

MOVING

PACKING

You might enjoy a stick in the eye more than moving, but these tips will keep you from looking like a pirate.

START EARLY

Pack and clean early, especially if you have friends helping you move. They won't be amused when they show up to load the truck and you haven't disassembled your bed yet.

BOXES ARE EXPENSIVE

(Often $5 per box.) If you buy them directly from the movers, they're even more expensive [insert evil laughter from moving company here]. Have a chat with your friendly grocery store owner to see if any boxes are being thrown away.

LABEL THE OUTSIDE OF YOUR BOXES

You'll be glad later.

PURGE

Get rid of the stuff you no longer need or want beforehand. Donate that hideous casserole dish that you've always hated and never use.

PACK WITH CLOTHES

Rather than buying packing peanuts, wrap fragile items in clean clothing.

PACK HEAVY OBJECTS IN SMALLER BOXES.

Tempting though it is to place all your dishes and kitchenware in The Biggest Box, you risk hurting your back and breaking the box.

TRIPLE-CHECK

Check every drawer, nook, and cranny before leaving your current place. You don't want the next tenant getting the pirate treasure that you hid and forgot.

RENT A MOVING TRUCK

NEGOTIATE

Do not accept your first quote. Each rental company wants your business and will slash its prices to get it. Call everyone, get your best quote, and then try to get the other companies to improve. Use the line, "I'd really prefer to go with you, but..."

TALK TO THE LOCAL OFFICE

You'll initially speak to the national office to get a quote. The national office can guarantee you a rate, but usually cannot guarantee you a truck (bizarre). Call your local office to confirm that you have a truck.

RESERVE EARLY

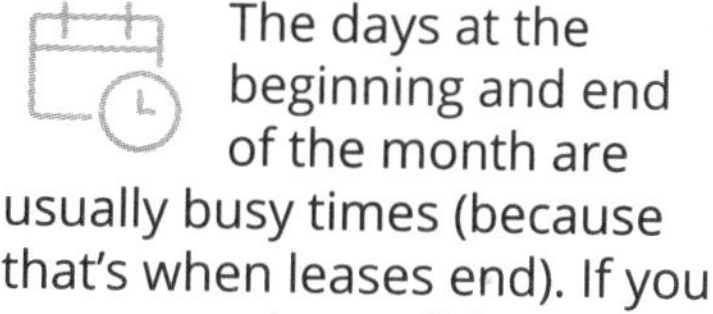

The days at the beginning and end of the month are usually busy times (because that's when leases end). If you reserve early, you'll have more options and better pricing.

CHECK INSURANCE

The boxes that you pack yourself are usually not insured in the move.

OTHER STUFF

UPDATE YOUR ADDRESS

Notify everyone—your doctor's office, your soon-to-be-previous employer, utilities, your bank and credit card companies—of your new address. Visit USPS.com at least two weeks ahead to forward your mail.

CHECK YOUR UTILITIES

Give your current and future utilities lots of notice. Schedule service in your new place before you move in so you can watch a movie after you unpack.

CHECK LOCKS

For your next apartment, confirm with your landlord that your locks have been changed so the previous tenant doesn't have access to your place.

RENTER'S INSURANCE

OVERVIEW

Renter's insurance is for any of you who rent the roof over your head, whether it's a house or an apartment.

Your landlord or condo association may have insurance, but this only protects only the building, not your things in it.

Renter's insurance protects your personal property against fire, theft, and vandalism (usually wherever you take it). You'll also be protected if someone gets hurt on your property. (This is called liability protection.)

The price for renter's insurance is usually based on four things:

Dollar amount of coverage
The amount you think all of your stuff is worth.

Deductible
What you pay out of your own pocket before your insurance kicks in.

Actual cash value or replacement cost
If you paid $400 for a new couch, $400 is your replacement cost. Once it's covered in ketchup stains and smells like cat pee, the actual cash value might be more like $.35.

Location and previous claims
If you live in an area where you (or even your neighbors) get your bike stolen every week, you'll probably end up paying more for your policy.

STORY TIME

When Alex's apartment burned down and investigators asked what was lost, Alex hesitated. "Um," they said, trying to get as much as possible for the lost items,

"I HAD A 60-INCH PLASMA TV, A GUCCI SALAD SPINNER, THREE FABERGE EGGS, A BEARSKIN RUG MADE OUT OF CHEWBACCA ..."

Alex went on and on, piling up $36 million worth of claims.

The investigators eyed Alex suspiciously and handed them a pamphlet titled

"INSURANCE FRAUD."

Alex called the investigators and explained that they had made a mistake and that all of those items were in their OTHER one-bedroom apartment. Their actual compensation ended up being $918.42 and a life outside of prison.

SETTING UP WI-FI

TERMS

Wi-Fi. The oxygen of life (sorta). On campus, Wi-Fi is a given, but when you're on your own, the internet is all up to you. Here's a few tips on getting it all set up.

ISP

Your **INTERNET SERVICE PROVIDER** is the company you pay for your internet. Without these guys, the town library would still be the cool place to hang.

MODEMS AND ROUTERS

To oversimplify (you're welcome), your **MODEM** turns the information you receive from your ISP into the glorious internet for your computer, tv, phone, etc. If you have more than one device in your place that needs oxygen, you'll need a **ROUTER** (usually wireless) to route your internet to your computer, tv, phone, etc.

MESH NETWORK

If you've got a lot of Wi-Fi dead spots (places you can't connect) or you're living in a 3,000+ square foot pad, you can buy a **MESH NETWORK**, multiple "points" (little devices) that transmit your Wi-Fi better. But as long as your place isn't really big, you should be OK without one.

TIPS

FEES

Don't rent the modem offered by your ISP. Buy one yourself to save the monthly fee. You can even buy a modem/router combo (not as good as a pizza/ wing combo, but a close second).

If your place is not already wired for the internet, you may get an installation fee (and a hole drilled in your wall by your service provider). Oh, joy!

SPEED

Don't overpay for crazy-fast internet speed. 25 mbps is enough for streaming movies. If you connect to lots of devices or play online games, you may need a faster speed (e.g., 200+ mbps), but you can always upgrade if you have a need for more speed.

SECURITY

If you want your neighbors to think twice before trying to use your Wi-Fi network, pick a name like "C:Virus.exe" or "FBI Surveillance Van #21."

BASIC HOME FIXES

TIPS

For big fixes, call your landlord or plumber. But for small problems, you may be able to fix them yourself in a minute.

MY ROOMMATE CLOGGED THE TOILET

Avert your eyes. Then grab a plunger, the thing with a long handle and a large rubber cup at the end. Put the rubber cup over the drain opening. Repeatedly push and pull on the handle for about 20 seconds.

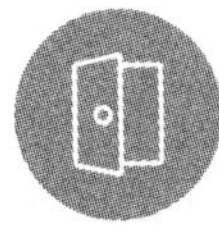

MY DOOR SQUEAKS

Whip out some Vaseline or WD-40 and coat any squeaky metal bits that are giving you problems.

TIPS

MY LIGHTS WENT OUT

Maybe it's an impromptu rave. But if a DJ doesn't strut out, look for your fuse box (usually on the wall of a bedroom closet or hallway). Inside you should see a set of bulky looking on/off switches (**CIRCUIT BREAKERS**). If a breaker is "tripped" to the off position, something may have sent it too much electrical zap. Turn the switch back on. If this doesn't do the trick, you may need to replace a blown fuse. (Call your landlord.)

MY GARBAGE DISPOSAL DOESN'T WORK

Turn it on.

***Don't* hear a sound?** Check under the sink to see if the disposal is plugged in. Press the red reset button on the bottom. Check your fuse box for a tripped circuit breaker.

***Do* hear a sound?** Turn off the disposal (very important) and stick your hand down the drain to feel for obstructions, like a spoon. Or insert an Allen wrench in the hole under the disposal unit and turn.

MY DRAIN IS CLOGGED

Get the landlord's permission before trying to fix a clogged drain. There may be reasons they don't want you sticking things down there. If you get the OK, slowly pour boiling water down the drain. If this doesn't help, straighten out a regular coat hanger to create a small hook, and stick it into the drain to fish for hair and other gunk. If this hair problem continues, you could shave your roommate's head, but ask first.

BUYING PAINT

OVERVIEW

It's time to paint your kitchen. You decide on the color blue and confidently head to your local paint store.

When you walk in, you say, "I'll take blue." And the clerk replies, "Would you like an interior oil-based semigloss?" And you say, "No, I'd like bluuuuuuee."

Well, a long time ago, someone decided to make paint complicated. We'll help you make sense of it all.

First, paints fall into two basic categories:

LATEX (OR WATER-BASED)

Most of the paint is water, so it dries quickly and is easy on cleanup. It's the most common type of paint and retains its color better than oil-based paint over time.

OIL-BASED

As you might guess, most of the paint is oil. It usually goes on smoother and covers more thoroughly in one coat, but it's harder to clean up and it stinks.

OVERVIEW

Next you have to pick your color. Unfortunately, "blue" comes in about 10 billion different shades.

You'll be given some choices (displayed on a small card, or **SWATCH**) to help you decide.

If the color "Dreaming of Clouds" speaks to your heart, then by all means, follow your heart. Are you nervous that your heart might lead you astray? Buy a sample size of paint, slap some on a surface, and decide whether you like it.

Your paint store won't have all 10 billion choices on the shelf. Instead, your dream color will get mixed for you while you wait.

Your next step is to pick the right type of **FINISH**. Each color has five different degrees of shininess (see the arrow on the right). A gloss is easier to clean, so it may be good for a kitchen. A flat finish does not reflect too much light, so it may be a good choice for a ceiling.

Finally, if you're painting on drywall or making a big change in colors, you may need to apply a **PRIMER** (an undercoat to help your paint bond) before you paint. Yes! More work!

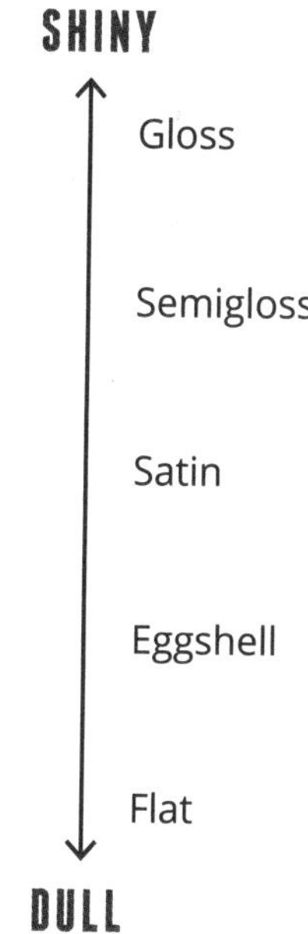

CLEANING YOUR PLACE

OVERVIEW

Since *Snow White* has a monopoly on the local deer, squirrel, and raccoon population for low-cost housecleaning services, you may be forced to do your own.

GET AN ALL-PURPOSE CLEANER

This stuff is good for almost everything. Look for all-natural sprays and wipes in a scent you like (since you'll be smelling it).

AVOID MIXING CLEANING PRODUCTS

As a general rule, never mix household cleaners. The combination of certain chemicals can be highly toxic.

SCHEDULE

BATHROOMS EVERY 1–2 WEEKS

Start here, because once you're done, everything else in your place is easy.

Toilet: Spray with toilet bowl cleaner, wait for a few minutes, then clean with a brush. Use your all-purpose cleaner on the rim and lid and wipe it all down.

Sink: This is the toilet's cleaner cousin and, like it, a Jacuzzi for germs. Whip out your all-purpose cleaner and spray all around the sink. Wipe and you're done.

Tub/shower: They clean you every day, so return the favor to them. Use your all-purpose cleaner again and wipe/rub until they whistle in joy.

SCHEDULE

Tile grout: Does your shower have tiles with a pretty green color between them? *This area should not be green.* Add some grout cleaner and scrub with a toothbrush (not your roommate's).

DUST EVERY 4 WEEKS

This stuff is bad for your lungs. Put a sock over your hand and give everything a hand hug. Baseboards, cabinets, and blinds should all get the same treatment.

REFRIGERATOR EVERY 3 MONTHS

First, remove everything from your refrigerator, as you don't want cleaning chemicals touching your food. Then use your all-purpose cleaner again to wipe stuff down.

KITCHEN SURFACES EVERY 1–2 WEEKS

Kitchen surfaces need a good wipedown every 1–2 weeks (for spilled mayonnaise, even sooner). Your all-purpose cleaner is still your friend. Use it.

VACUUM EVERY 1–2 WEEKS

Do this last, as lots of dust will end up on the floor. If your vacuum bag is full, empty it; otherwise, your vacuum will actually be a move-your-dust-around-your-place machine. And emptying your bag is insanely satisfying.

OVEN EVERY 6 MONTHS

Grease and grime buildup can affect your oven's performance, create smoke, and lead to a risk of fire. Remove the racks and clean them separately with warm water and dishwashing liquid. For the oven itself, use an oven cleaner and follow the product directions.

BEDDING EVERY 1–2 WEEKS

It doesn't take long for bedding to collect dust mites, skin cells, and oils. Most bedding can and should be washed in a washing machine.

THROW OUT EXPIRED FOODS

Right now, in the back of your fridge, something is lurking behind your leftovers. Take a few minutes every week to throw out foods that are past their prime.

FOOD SAFETY

OVERVIEW

Since you might be cooking for yourself more, you should know how to avoid self-inflicted food poisoning.

STAY CLEAN

Wash your hands before and after cooking, and keep your food prep area clean. Don't touch your phone while you're cooking, because every germ in the world currently lives on your phone.

BE CAREFUL OF RAW MEAT

Bacteria live on raw meat (including poultry and fish). Keep raw meat in a separate plastic bag from the grocery store and in your refrigerator to help prevent cross-contamination. Use a separate cutting board for meat, and don't wash raw meat, since bacteria will spread. Always use a food thermometer to confirm meat is thoroughly cooked (check online for meat-specific temps).

WASH VEGGIES

Raw veggies, especially leafy greens, are the most common sources of dangerous pathogens (bad things). Rinse them under running water.

STAY OUT OF THE DANGER ZONE

The temperature "danger zone" is 41° to 135° F, which is completely different from the *Top Gun* danger zone (although both are dangerous).

OVERVIEW

When food is in the danger zone, bacteria spreads in that food, which can become unsafe to eat within hours. Refrigerate food promptly. Your fridge should be set to no higher than 40° F.

THAW FOOD SAFELY

Yes, your food will thaw much faster if you let it sit out on the counter. Unfortunately, that's also how you grow an army of bacteria ready to take on Sparta, and then your gut. Thaw foods in the fridge, under cold running water, or in a microwave.

AVOID HARMFUL FOODS

Avoid unpasteurized milk and cheese (harmful bacteria) and raw eggs (salmonella risk). Harmful things are harmful.

CHECK PACKAGING

Damaged packaging may be a bad sign. Also check expiration dates and throw out expired foods.

REPLACE SPONGES

Sponges and dishcloths should be sanitized and replaced frequently. Sanitize sponges every other day by wetting them and then microwaving them for a minute on high. Replace them every week or two.

SECTION FIVE:

MONEY

"After FICA, Social Security, and federal and state taxes, your allowance comes to 18 cents."

INTEREST

THE RULE OF MONEY

A few easy decisions with your money can earn you hundreds of extra dollars each year in interest. This is easy money, so read on.

Let's talk about the basics. Granted, this stuff is very simple, but it sets a good foundation for later. The **RULE OF MONEY** (that's what we'll call it) says:

WHEN YOU USE SOMEONE ELSE'S MONEY, YOU HAVE TO PAY FOR IT.

For example, when you make a deposit in the bank, the bank uses your money. It has to pay for that money. It pays you interest.

When you borrow money to pay for college, you are using someone else's money. You have to pay for it. You pay your lender interest.

The most important thing to understand is that the "interest" you *earn* is the same kind of interest as the "interest" you *pay* (simple enough).

Put another way, the relationship goes both ways. You earn interest when someone else uses your money, and you pay interest for the use of someone else's money.

Now you're certainly "interested." *Ba-dum ching!* Thanks, folks, you've been a lovely audience. Don't forget to tip your server.

MOVE YOUR MONEY

Look at all the places where you're *earning* interest (e.g., savings accounts) and all the places where you're *paying* interest (e.g., credit cards). Then compare all of your different interest rates.

YOU SHOULD MOVE YOUR MONEY TO THE HIGHEST INTEREST RATE.

If your credit card charges you 18%, but you earn only 2% on your money market fund, pay off your credit card debt from your money market fund. A rate of 18% is highest.

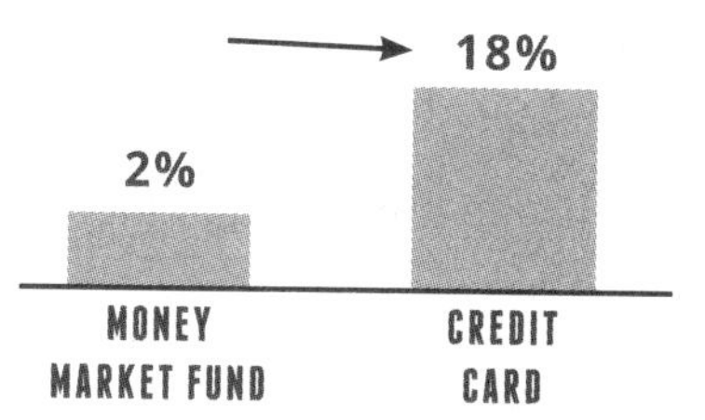

If your car loan charges you 2%, but you earn 5% on your money market fund, add money to your money market fund instead of paying off your car loan. A rate of 5% is highest.

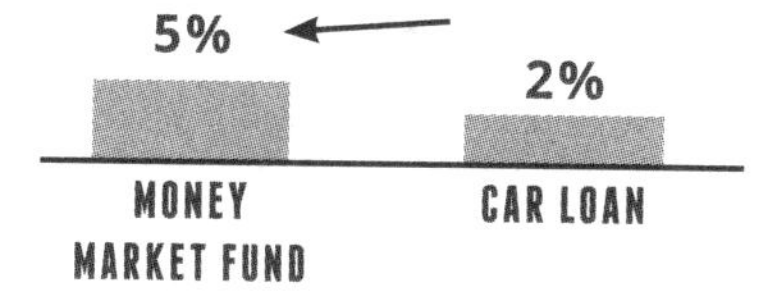

You may need to consider taxes and other factors, but these smart, easy choices will almost always put more money in your pocket.

WHO CARES?

You may be thinking,

"2% ... 3% ... 6% ... WHAT'S THE BIG DEAL?"

CONSIDER THIS

If you invest $1,000 in something that pays you 6% versus 2%, you'll earn $60 by the end of the year versus $20.

You are not doing any work to earn this extra money, except simply making a decision about where to put it. If someone offered you $40 for doing nothing, wouldn't you take it?

CHECKING ACCOUNTS

OVERVIEW

Everybody loves checking accounts, but here's the problem: basic checking accounts usually pay **0% interest**.

The bank gets to use your money but doesn't pay you for it. As you now know, that is *not fair.* The **RULE OF MONEY** states:

WHEN YOU USE SOMEONE ELSE'S MONEY, YOU HAVE TO PAY FOR IT.

A checking account is using your money and not paying for it. That's breaking the **RULE**.

To make matters worse, checking accounts often charge you a monthly fee. Let's get this straight: you pay the fee, and they use your money? That's not fair.

SUMMARY

PROS

- You have easy access to your money.
- You can write checks.
- You can go to ATMs.

CONS

- You may earn zero interest.
- You might be charged fees.

CONCLUSION

Everybody needs to write a check or visit an ATM once in a while to get cash. Checking accounts serve a purpose. So search for banks that offer the highest interest rates on their checking accounts.

But then keep only enough money in there to cover your checks and to avoid fees for falling below any minimum balance.

SAVINGS ACCOUNTS

OVERVIEW

Savings accounts *sound* good, but once you get past the surface, there isn't a whole lot of substance there.

Here's why: basic savings accounts pay squat. Uncle Sam may guarantee your money, but a savings account usually only pays you tiny interest. Think tiny. Now split that in half until it is micro-tiny.

Tiny interest is better than zero interest from the bully checking accounts, but you have better alternatives (see our topic on **MONEY MARKET FUNDS**).

SUMMARY

PROS

- You have easy access to your money.
- You can go to ATMs.

CONS

- You earn little interest.

CONCLUSION

Savings accounts can be a reservoir —a holding place to stash some cash until you decide what you want to do with it. It's just a little bit better than hiding your money under your mattress.

CDs

OVERVIEW

You're probably thinking to yourself, "CDs? I *love* the Chunichi Dragons. Daisuke Sobue is *such* a dreamboat." No, we're talking about **CERTIFICATES OF DEPOSIT**. These are places you invest your money for *set periods of time.*

PRISON (MINUS THE DEMENTORS)

Each CD has a set lifespan (3 months up to 10 years) with a set interest rate. When you put your money in a CD, you have to keep it there. Your money is in prison with no visiting hours. You can't even use FaceTime.

For example, if you put $1,000 into a one-year CD at 3%, you'll be guaranteed to earn $30 interest after a year. You lock in the 3% rate.

If you take your money out early, you'll get whacked with a big penalty (which negates the reason for having put your money in a CD in the first place).

HIGHER INTEREST

You are rewarded for putting your money in prison by earning more interest than from ordinary savings accounts.

OVERVIEW

The rates will change according to the length of the prison sentence.

Usually, the longer the sentence, the higher the interest rate. Rates can vary widely from bank to bank, so shop around using rate comparison websites. Find a cushy holding cell for your Benjamins.

DECISIONS

If you need access to your money, avoid CDs. Coming out of school, you may have a lot of initial expenses and need access to cash. The minimum deposit for a CD is usually around $1,000, but this amount varies from bank to bank.

SUMMARY

PROS

- Usually better rates than checking or savings accounts.
- You lock in your rate.
- Usually guaranteed by the government.

CONS

- Your money is in prison.
- You pay penalties for taking your money out early.

CONCLUSION

If you don't need your money for a set period of time and you want to lock in a rate, a CD might be a good, safe option for storing your cash. Just make sure that you won't need this money during its prison term.

MONEY MARKET FUNDS

OVERVIEW

Money market funds have many benefits over savings accounts.

HIGH RATES

Money market funds often pay higher interest rates than savings accounts, and occasionally higher than CDs.

EASY ACCESS

Your money is never in prison, like when you invest in a CD. You may not be able to use an ATM to get your money, but many money market funds allow you to zap your money into your checking account in a day's time for no fee.

CHECK WRITING

With many money market funds, you can often even write checks.

Is this financial utopia? Pretty close. There are a couple of minor drawbacks. Read on.

RATES MOVE AROUND

You may put your money into the fund when it's earning 2%, but after six months, the rate may drop to 1% or jump to 3%. You cannot lock in your rate. However, these rates are still usually higher than savings account rates.

OVERVIEW

NO GOVERNMENT GUARANTEE

The government does not guarantee money market funds, so theoretically, you could lose your money. But virtually no US money market fund has ever lost money. You can't find a much safer investment.

BIG CHECKS

If you write a check, it usually has to be a BIG check (often $250 or more). When you need to pay rent or make a loan payment, a money market fund is perfect. For making smaller purchases, you'll still need a checking account.

MINIMUM DEPOSITS

Some money market funds require a $1,000+ minimum deposit to open an account.

NOT AT BANKS

You usually can't get money market funds at your local bank. Banks may offer something called money market accounts, but those often pay the same rates as savings accounts (ask your bank for all of its high-interest-rate options).

You can open a money market fund from an online broker or a mutual fund family.

SUMMARY

PROS

- Better rates than other low-risk investments.
- You can write checks.
- Your investment is safe.

CONS

- Rates move.
- You typically have to write big checks.
- Require minimum investment.

CONCLUSION

They're a good place to safely invest your money.

STOCKS AND BONDS

STOCKS

When you buy the stock of a company, you're actually buying part of that company (but don't expect to own the corner office with the nice view). You own a small, small sliver. If you buy 10 bazillion shares, you own a medium-sized sliver.

If the company does well, the stock will probably do well, and you'll be able to buy yourself a new smartphone. If the CEO of the company is a crook and drains the company dry, then you may have to visit the local pawnshop and try to get your money back. So, owning a stock implies part ownership in a company with all of the pros and cons.

STOCK RISKS

Savings accounts and money market funds are relatively safe places to put your money.

Stocks, on the other hand, come with the real risk of losing money—and not just your 2% or 6% interest. Your entire investment could go into the toilet.

But if you buy a mix of stocks of great companies and hold them for the *long run*, the stock market has historically been a great investment.

A famous investor named Ben Graham once said, "In the *short run*, the market is a voting machine, but in the *long run*, it is a weighing machine." In other words, tomorrow stocks will rise and fall based on the news and random opinions. But over many years, the stocks of great companies typically do well.

STOCK RISKS

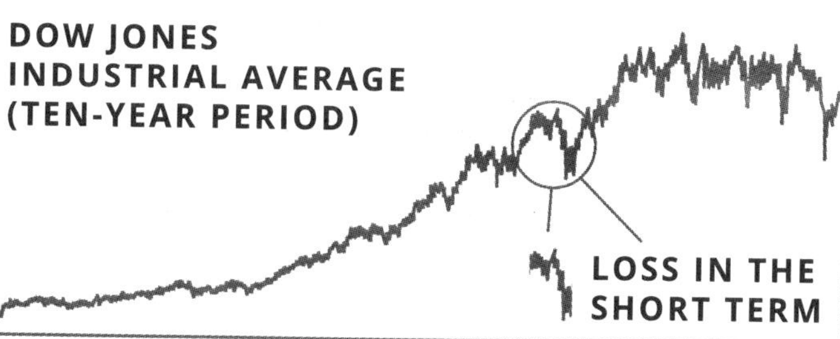

The key is picking a *mix of stocks* of *great companies* over the *long run* (easier said than done).

On the left, you can see that if you had invested in a mix of stocks (the Dow Jones index) for a decade, you'd have been a winner.

But even during this 10-year "up" period, you could have easily lost your money during *short* periods of time.

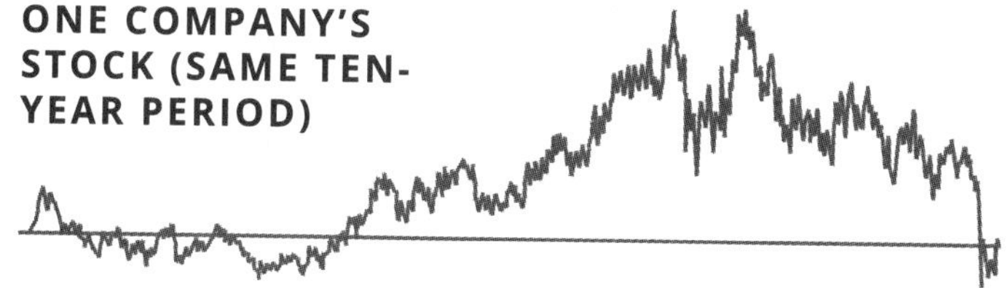

Additionally, had you invested in a *single stock* during this "up" decade, you could have lost money.

Individual stocks or short-term investments can leave you poor and sad.

BUYING STOCKS

You can buy stocks from lots of "online brokerages" (search the web). Shop around. Thankfully, there's a lot of competition, and fees for each transaction can vary dramatically. Often, you'll find a trade-off between price and the availability of stock research information.

If you invest for the short term, be willing to handle large price swings in your investment.

Bored yet? See the last page of this book.

STOCK SURE BETS

•

•

•

•

•

•

•

•

•

STOCK EXPECTATIONS

Also be aware that stock prices are largely driven by **expectations**, among other things. If you find a company that you feel is strong or weak, determine whether your opinions have already been factored into the price of the stock.

Many stocks fall, even when the company reports positive earnings (every quarter, companies announce how things are going), because expectations for the company's earnings were even higher than the earnings actually reported.

BONDS

Bonds aren't discussed as much in the news, but they're important to understand.

BONDS ARE IOUS.

When a company or government (like the US government) needs a little extra money, it issues bonds (or IOUs) to get some cash.

In our **INTEREST** topic, the **RULE OF MONEY** states: when you use someone else's money, you have to pay for it.

These companies or governments need to pay back their money with interest. So how much interest do they have to pay?

That all depends on you: at what rate would you feel comfortable enough to give up your money with the chance of not getting it back? Your answer should depend on *who* is borrowing your money.

If you lend your money to Uncle Sam (the US government), you should feel pretty confident that you'll get your money back.

Suppose your cousin starts a company that sells gift wrapping that bears a striking resemblance to yesterday's newspaper. (Think about this for a second.) You might not feel as safe giving money to your cousin's company, which might go belly-up in a month.

In order to give up your money to your cousin, you'd need to get paid a higher interest rate to feel comfortable.

In a nutshell, that's how bonds work. Safe borrowers (like Uncle Sam) issue bonds for low rates, whereas riskier companies or governments (like your cousin) issue IOUs for higher rates of interest.

When you buy a bond mutual fund (see our next topic), determine whether these bonds are issued by safe or by sketchy companies. Bonds can rise and fall—just like stocks. So don't just lend your money to anyone.

MUTUAL FUNDS

OVERVIEW

A mutual fund is just a whole bunch of stocks, bonds, or somethings put into a nice little bundle.

For instance, one fund might be a bunch of food or tech stocks.

Imagine if your folks secretly owned and ran a huge mutual fund company (another reason to be nice to them). They might have a Food Fund or a Tech Fund. Each fund would invest only in food or technology companies. You'd never really know which stocks were in each fund at any given time, because fund investments continually change.

Mutual funds are often considered "safer" than individual stocks, because when some stocks in a fund go down, others may go up to offset them.

The important thing to remember is that when you buy a mutual fund, you are allowing someone else (a mutual fund manager) to make your investment decisions for you.

If this section is boring you, please refer to the last page in the book.

STORY TIME

Picking stocks is a lot like picking horses. So we'll tell a horse-track story.

Once upon a time, our good friend Alex went to the Kentucky Derby to watch some horses run around a track.

Alex looked in the program, through mounds of confusing information, and then picked a horse named Ocean Cookie because the name sounded cool. (Word of advice: Don't pick stocks because the name sounds cool.) Occasionally, Alex picked the first horse that peed before the race, because it made the horse "lighter."

Alex continued to use these sophisticated gambling methods until his horses lost the first three races.

Obviously, something wasn't working.

Then Alex noticed a flier on the wall for a website that offered a "Racetrack Pick of the Week!" for a $20/month subscription.

Buying a mutual fund is like subscribing to this horse-picking website. You're paying someone else to pick your investments for you. The site might make you money, but it might not. You pay a monthly fee either way. The same holds true for mutual funds.

You pay a mutual fund manager to pick some stocks for you. Your manager might be right. Or might not. But you're going to pay a fee for the advice either way.

MUTUAL FUND FEES

As we mentioned, mutual fund companies need to make their fees. Many times these fees are called **LOADS**. A mutual fund may charge you a front-end load or a back-end load.

FRONT-END LOADS

These fees are charged to you before the race even gets started. Assume that the load is 2%. If you give $1,000 to invest, you lose $20 before the race starts. Avoid them.

BACK-END LOADS

These fees charged when you withdraw your money from the fund. Avoid these fees, too.

You don't have to buy load funds. In fact, there's no evidence that funds with loads perform better than funds with no loads.

MUTUAL FUND FEES

But of course, you have to be charged somewhere. That's where the expense ratio comes in. (Almost all funds charge this.) After all, fund managers need money to pay for their kids' braces just like everyone else (unless their spouse is an orthodontist, but whatever).

EXPENSE RATIO

This is a pay-as-you-go fee, much like the monthly website subscription from our story. If a fund has a 2% annual expense ratio, you'll pay that expense only for the number of days your money is in the fund. If you own the fund for half a year, you'll get charged only half the fee, or 1%.

BUYING FUNDS

You can purchase mutual funds through online brokers (companies that sell lots of investment products) or directly from a mutual fund family.

When making your decisions, keep in mind that mutual funds are often romanticized as great investments, because some smart person invests your money for you, and because you're buying a mix of stocks.

When you buy a technology fund, you're still investing in technology stocks. If all technology stocks go down (which, amazingly, has been known to happen), your fund also will go down.

Don't be lulled into a false sense of security just because you have a fund manager on your side.

FUND CHOICES

When you buy a mutual fund, these terms will help:

GROWTH FUNDS

These funds are usually composed of companies that still have growth potential.

INCOME FUNDS

The companies in these funds are more established and make periodic payments.

BALANCED FUNDS

These funds mix stocks and bonds.

INDEXES AND ETFs

OVERVIEW

Let's say you want to buy some mutual funds, but you don't know which group of stocks, or sector, to put them in. Food? Technology? Who knows?

You may want to invest in a broad mix of stocks, because as we mentioned in the **STOCKS AND BONDS** topic, the general market usually does well over time.

HOW DO YOU DO THIS?

For starters, it's difficult to keep track of every stock in the world (for most of us), so when people refer to "the market," they usually mean one of the indexes on the next page. The Dow Jones, NASDAQ, and S&P 500 are often used in the news to describe the whole market.

OVERVIEW

INDEX	DESCRIPTION	BIG STOCKS	ETF
Dow Jones Industrial Avg.	30 of the biggest companies in the US	Disney, Coca-Cola, Nike	DIA (Diamonds)
NASDAQ	5,000+ companies (many in technology)	Apple, Amazon, Microsoft	QQQQ (for NASDAQ 100)
S&P 500	500 widely held companies	Apple, Facebook, Alphabet (Google)	SPY (SPDRs = "Spiders")

You've probably seen these names in the news a lot. If not, read the news.

To invest in an index, you can do one of two things:

- Buy an index mutual fund.
- Buy an ETF (exchange-traded fund).

An **INDEX MUTUAL FUND** is a fund that mimics the performance of an index. If the index rises 1%, your fund will rise 1% (minus some fees). The company Vanguard has been the pioneer of low-cost index funds.

An **ETF** does the same thing, but usually with lower fees.

The DIA, QQQQ, and SPY are like stocks that track different indexes. These ETFs can be purchased like any other stock from an online broker.

If you're looking for an easy way to invest in the general market with minimal fees, an ETF (DIA, QQQQ, or SPY) is a good start.

CREDIT

OVERVIEW

Credit is your ability to borrow money; it shows the trust others have that you'll pay it back. Credit is important in many areas of your life, like credit cards, auto loans, mortgages, apartment leases, and more. When you make a big purchase, credit is often involved.

NOW VS. LATER

Buying things on credit (borrowing money) is a *now versus later decision*. You'll get the thing *now*, but you'll have less money *later* because you've paid interest on your purchases.

Buying too many things on credit is like carrying around a leaky bucket. As water (interest) leaks out of your bucket (your savings), you'll have less to spend down the road.

CREDIT SCORE

Your credit score is a number from 300–850 that tells lenders your likelihood of paying them back. The higher your score, the better you look to your lender. Your score is based on your repayment history, number of open accounts, and total debt.

CREDIT REPORT

A credit report is basically your financial transcript. Big Brother keeps track of all your financial dealings for the rest of the world to see. Request a free report annually from AnnualCreditReport.com or order one online from one of three credit reporting sites (Equifax, Experian, or Transunion).

Credit reports are also helpful to watch for the bad folks who want to take a loan out in your name. Read our topic on **IDENTITY THEFT**.

SAMPLE CREDIT REPORT

PERSONAL DATA

Louise Pindleberry Branford, CT 06405	Social Security Number: xxx-45-2121 Date of Birth: 2/19/1999

EMPLOYMENT HISTORY

Happy Hospital	Location: Erie, PA	Employment Date: 2/12/2020	Verified Date: 4/4/2021

PUBLIC HISTORY

No bankruptcies on file.
No liens on file.

CREDIT INFORMATION

Company Name	Acct Number & Whose Acct	Date Opened	Last Activity	Type of Acct and Status	High Credit	Items as of Date Reported	Past Due	Date Reported
Capital Two	412654460 JOINT ACCT	02/2019	4/2021	Revolving PAY AS AGREED	$800	16	$600	2/2021

PRIOR PAYING HISTORY

30 days past due 03 times; 60 days past due 02 times; 90+ days past due 00 times

MINIMUM PAYMENTS

A lender (e.g., the bank that issues your credit card) makes its money from collecting interest payments from you. Generally speaking, the longer you take to pay back your balance, the more you pay in interest.

For example, many credit cards offer you a low minimum payment each month to *encourage* you to keep a balance on your card. For example, if you have a balance of $4,000, your minimum monthly payment may be only $83.33.

Account Summary

	Previous Balance	(+)Purchases & Advances	(-)Payments	(-)Credits	(+)Finance Charge	(+)Late Charges	(=)New Balance
Purchases	1825.61	4183.99	2000.00	9.60			4000.00
Advances							
Total	1825.61	4183.99	2000.00	9.60			4000.00

Purchases Minimum Due	83.33
Advances Minimum Due	
Amount Over Credit Line	
Other ways to rip you off	
Past Due	
Minimum Amount Due	83.33

Rate Summary Number of days this Billing Period 31	Purchases	Advances
Calculation Method	Daily	Daily
Periodic Rate	.05041%	.05476%
Nominal Annual Percentage Rate	18.400%	19.990%
Annual Percentage Rate	18.400%	19.990%
Balance Subject to Finance Charge		

MANAGING YOUR CREDIT

Some surprising math

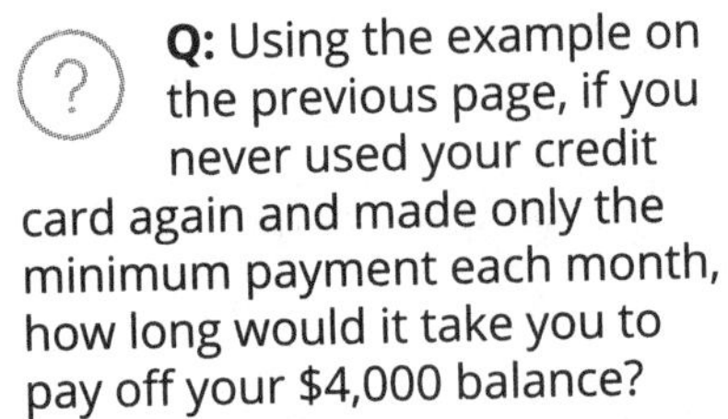

Q: Using the example on the previous page, if you never used your credit card again and made only the minimum payment each month, how long would it take you to pay off your $4,000 balance?

A: Roughly 29 years and $13,000 later, you'd pay off your balance. As a general rule, *try to pay your entire credit card balance every month.*

Live within your paycheck. No, duh. But when the iPhone 46 comes out with BodySend (human teleportation) for only $9,999, how can you resist?

"THE MONTHLY"

Beware of "the monthly." Many high-ticket items (cars, electronics, etc.) are pitched by their low monthly costs.

WHICH SOUNDS LIKE THE BETTER DEAL?

(a) $500 per month

(b) $12,000 now

Based on the above, the answer is, "Who knows?" As in, who knows how many months you'll be paying?

When you purchase that fancy, diamond-encrusted moped on a monthly basis, you're buying it on credit (**FINANCING**). Buried deep within the fine print, you'll find your interest rate.

If you pay $500 for 36 months, you'll end up paying $18,000. The extra $6,000 you pay over 36 months is the cost for paying over time (interest).

Do the fancy math.

MONTHLY PAYMENT

X

MONTHS

$$$

and then make your decision. If you can, pay up front to save money. Or you could buy a really fancy *bike* instead.

BAD CREDIT SCORES

Sadly, there's no magical cure for bad credit. Credit problems stay on your record for seven years (10 years for bankruptcies). If you have damaged your credit score for one reason or another, it can be repaired. However, it will take time and perseverance.

In the meantime, beware of snake oil sales reps that guarantee they have magic erasers that will wipe away stains on your report. Remember that low score on your calculus exam? Unfortunately, you couldn't get that erased, either. The best thing to do is create a repayment plan now and stick with it.

CONSOLIDATE TO LOW RATES

Combine all of your balances on one card—the one with the lowest interest rate. Many cards offer a low (temporary) introductory teaser rate as an incentive to move your balance to their card. Take them up on their offer, and save yourself some money in interest payments.

Consolidating your credit debt into one account prevents you from making further purchases, because you have a smaller remaining credit line available to you. Plus, the credit police like to see that you have fewer spending opportunities. One monthly payment also simplifies your bill-paying.

MAKE A PLAN

Again, there's no magic plan for solving credit problems. Sit down and lay out all of your income and expenses. Give yourself a budget that will afford you the opportunity to pay off your balances.

CREDIT CARDS

OVERVIEW

Credit cards are sneaky little pieces of plastic. And they are very demanding when it comes to interest. They often charge more than 18%, which is higher than almost any other type of loan. Some also have an annual fee.

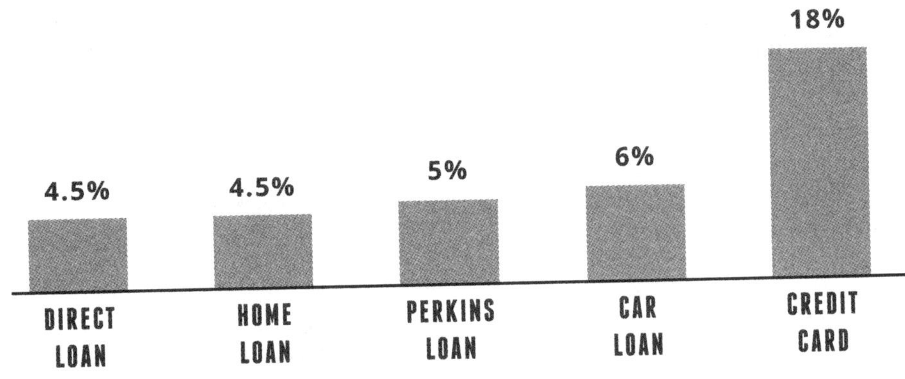

Too many people carry large balances on their credit cards and pay only the minimum balance due on each statement. Read our topic on **CREDIT** to learn more.

CREDIT CARD PERKS

But if you use credit cards wisely, they can include lots of perks.

BUILD YOUR CREDIT

Every time you buy something and pay it off quickly, the credit police put a gold star on your credit report (figuratively, of course). Your future landlord or bank lender likes to see those gold stars (literally).

FREE LOAN

When you purchase something with a credit card, you usually don't have to come up with the money for 15 to 30 days.

If you pay your bill (in full) on time, you're not charged any interest.

In our topic on **INTEREST**, you learned the **RULE OF MONEY**: When you use someone else's money, you have to pay for it. Now, in the case of credit cards, you're not playing by the rules. You're borrowing someone else's money for up to 30 days and not paying for it.

REWARDS

Many credit cards come with rewards, like cash back and frequent flier miles.

Many of these rewards cards charge an annual fee. If you spend more than $5,000 a year on a card with an annual fee of $50, the value of your rewards may outweigh the cost of the fee (that's good). If your purchases add up to a large amount each month, get yourself a card with rewards and pay off your monthly balance.

BIG DRAMATIC CONCLUSION ON CREDIT CARDS

If you're a human being (our target audience), you spend money. If you could get rewarded for charging the money you normally spend, why wouldn't you?

Apply for a credit card that pays rewards and get rid of those boring credit cards that do nothing for you. Ask it, What have you done for me lately?

Credit card companies charge merchants every single time a credit card purchase is made, whether online or in a store. If your bill is $10, the store may get only $9.70. The credit card company gets the other $0.30.

If the credit card company is willing to share some of its loot with you, why not take it?

Select a card that rewards you adequately. If your purchases are accumulating airline mileage points and you have taken a vow never to fly, maybe that card isn't for you.

Once you get a card with rewards, use your card for all of your *normal purchases*. Don't buy an unneeded pair of shoes simply because you want to rack up frequent flier miles. Rather, every time you purchase groceries, pay utilities, or buy gas or anything else, use your credit card with rewards and pay off your full credit card balance.

If you don't get squat for using cash or checks, why ever use them?

MORTGAGES

OVERVIEW

A home differs from almost anything else you'll ever buy. It will probably be the most expensive purchase you ever make. Unless you're Elon Musk.

First off, you may have to pony up only $15,000 for a $150,000 home. You can borrow the rest.

Can you see yourself walking into a department store, smacking down $15 for a $150 sweater, and saying, "Don't worry, I'll just borrow the rest"?

Second, you'll have a gajillion different ways to borrow the rest.

Can you see someone in the department store running up to you and yelling, "Hey, you can borrow the rest from me! Would you like an ARM, a 15- or 30-year fixed rate, or an FHA mortgage?" Uh...what?

Third, you can sometimes resell your home for more than you paid for it.

Can you imagine trying to resell your $150 sweater five years later for $200? Good luck. Try Goodwill.

Figuring out the finances on a home purchase can be confusing, but the choices you make here count a lot more than your choice of size of your fries and soda. We'll help you ask the right questions.

THE BASICS

So, what's a mortgage? Technically speaking, it's someone's right to your home if you don't make your payments. But technically speaking, that's really boring.

So, what's a **MORTGAGE**? For the rest of us, a mortgage is a fancy word for the loan you need to buy your home. If you can pay $15,000 for a $150,000 home, you'll need a $135,000 mortgage to make up the difference. Below are some words you'll see.

The **TERM**, or length, of a mortgage can vary. It's usually 15 or 30 years long (though you won't necessarily keep it that long). If mortgages were shorter, like five years, your monthly payments would be much, much larger.

Your **DOWN PAYMENT** is the money that comes out of your pocket to pay for your home. This can be anywhere from 0% to over 20% of your purchase price. Lenders want the borrower to have some skin in the game.

We previously learned in this chapter that when you use someone else's money, you have to pay for it. You'll pay interest here, too.

The interest rate and fees for your mortgage will vary from lender to lender, so it's a good idea to shop around. Visit local banks, contact a mortgage broker, or compare rates on rate comparison sites.

When comparing interest rates, be sure to compare the **APR**, or annual percentage rate. This rate will include all fees charged by your lender, allowing you to fairly compare different offers.

Once you finally reach your **CLOSING** (when you sign your papers), you'll have to pay a variety of closing costs.

CLOSING COSTS come in various shapes and colors. You may encounter points, discount points, application fees, credit report fees, appraisal fees, inspection fees, and so on. Yawn. Most of these will be due at your closing (on top of your down payment—yippee!). Your real estate agent will provide you a list of all of these costs before closing.

TYPES OF MORTGAGES

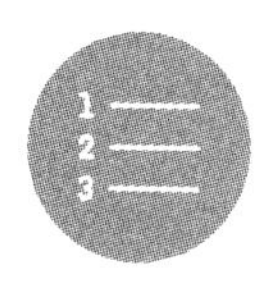

You'll have a choice amoung several types of mortgages. Your choice will determine how your monthly payment is calculated.

FIXED-RATE MORTGAGES

Your monthly payment stays the same every single month. Even if mortgage rates go up or down, your payment stays the same.

But, if rates drop a whole lot, you can refinance, which means that you can go to your lender and say: "Yuck! My rate is too high! I'd like to call a do-over and get the new, lower rate." You'll have to pay some fees to do this, but if the current rate is low enough, **REFINANCING** may well be worth it for you.

ADJUSTABLE-RATE MORTGAGES (ARMs)

Your payment will go up or down based on current interest rates.

You may hear of a 5/1 ARM or 10/1 ARM. This means that your rate is fixed for five or 10 years, but then it adjusts up or down every year after that.

ARMs are a little bit of a gamble. If you know that you'll be moving in five or 10 years, then you'll be finished paying on that particular house before the mortgage resets to a higher rate. But if you stay in your house for 20 years, you may find yourself making a much higher payment each month.

Tip: When you're applying for your mortgage, ask for "an ARM and a leg" with a straight face.

OH-SHOOT!-I-CAN'T-AFFORD-MY-PAYMENTS-ANYMORE MORTGAGES (OSICAMPAMs)

You may encounter a few crazy options that involve low initial payments that morph into much larger payments as time goes on (interest-only loans, balloons, and so on). Some of these can burn you over time, so make sure you understand all the terms of your mortgage before you sign on the dotted line.

THE DOWN PAYMENT HURDLE

One of the hardest things about buying a home is saving enough money for the down payment.

Why is a down payment so important? Suppose you borrowed $135,000 to buy a $150,000 home. Then suppose you ran off to a small village in Ecuador, never to be heard from again. Your lender would be upset. Your family would be furious.

Your lender would want its money back. If it then sold your house for only $140,000, the lender would still get all of its money back because of the "cushion" of your $15,000 down payment. But your family would still be furious.

Therefore, most lenders require that you make a down payment of at least 20%. If that's too steep, you'll probably have to purchase **MORTGAGE INSURANCE**. This can go by a number of different names (none of which we'd recommend as a name for your first child): PMI, MIP, and MMI.

By purchasing mortgage insurance, you may be allowed to put down as little as 5% of the purchase price. Plus, this fee can usually be included in your monthly mortgage payments.

If a 5% down payment is still too much, you many want to look into getting a **GOVERNMENT-BACKED** mortgage from the FHA (Federal Housing Authority).

Why would the government help you out? Well, Uncle Sam likes to promote homeownership.

You'll still have to pay for mortgage insurance, but an FHA loan allows you to purchase a home with as little as 3% down, and the interest rate can be lower than with traditional mortgages.

The FHA sets some standards for your house, neighborhood, and credit quality to determine if you're cool enough to qualify to sit at her lunch table.

Ask your broker about your options. Now you'll be armed with questions to ask.

EQUITY

Since you're reading this, you're probably interested in buying instead of renting a place. Why do so many people buy? There are many reasons, but one of the biggest is usually financial. When deciding, you should consider three things:

One, home prices often go up—no one's making any more land.

Two, part of your mortgage payments are tax deductible, unlike rent. Uncle Sam helps you out.

Three, when you make mortgage payments, some of your payment goes toward paying off your house. When you rent, you'll never see that money again (unless you're dating your landlord, but whatever).

This brings us to one of your favorite words (or one that soon will be):

which means "what's yours."

If you put $15,000 down to purchase a $150,000 home, $15,000 is yours. You have $15,000 in equity. Although you own the whole house, the rest of it isn't really "yours." If you sold your home tomorrow, you'd have to pay back the $135,000.

But here's the cool part: if the value of your home goes up by $5,000 (values frequently go up), all of this **APPRECIATION** is yours.

In fact, percentage-wise, this appreciation can often be pretty significant.

If you initially put down $15,000 and you make $5,000, your equity has appreciated by 33%. *Ka-ching*.

PAYMENTS ON A MORTGAGE

Now that you know about mortgages and equity, let's talk about your **MORTGAGE PAYMENTS**. You should know where your money is going.

Let's say you borrow $135,000 over 30 years at a fixed rate of 6%. (Did you ever think you'd read a sentence like that and keep reading? Well, buckle your seatbelt.)

Your mortgage payment will probably be due every month. When you make your payment, some of your money will be used to pay interest (remember: when you use someone else's money, you have to pay for it), and the rest will be used to pay off what you borrowed (the $135,000, or the **PRINCIPAL**).

The chart below is interesting (well, sort of interesting). In the first few years, the majority of each payment is used to pay interest.

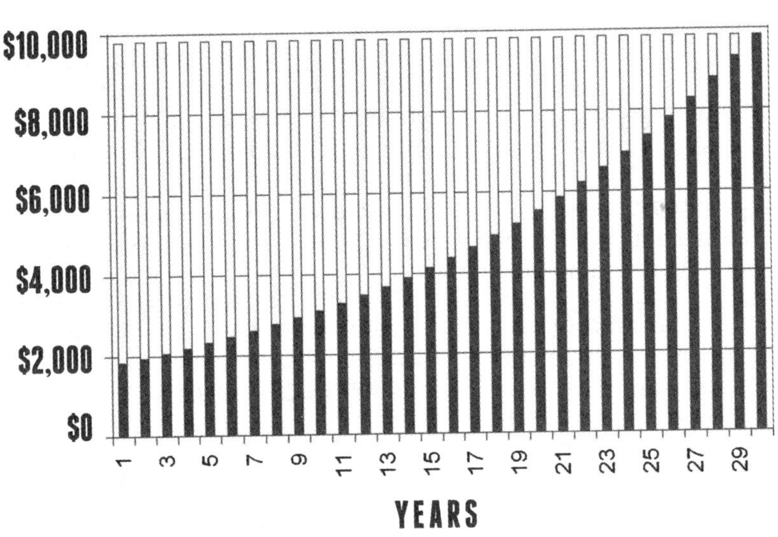

PAYMENTS ON A MORTGAGE

For example, in year one, you'll pay close to $8,000 of your $10,000 in payments for interest. The rest of your payment will pay down your principal (which becomes your equity). But over time, more and more of your payments go toward paying off your principal—and that's how you build equity.

WHY?

Well, at the beginning of your loan, you're paying interest on $135,000 (your whole loan). If you multiply this number by your 6% interest rate, you'll get about $8,000. (If you get a different number, remember to carry the three and the two—or use an app called "Calculator.")

The remainder of your payment ($2,000) pays down your principal.

But in year two, you'll be paying interest on less principal (since you paid $2,000 of it off in year one). So, more of your $10,000 yearly payment will go toward principal instead of interest.

How did we decide on the yearly payment number of $10,000? In our example, it's the number that results in a $0 balance on your mortgage after 30 years. Search the internet

for "mortgage calculator" to try this yourself. (Note: the first time you search for this, you'll officially become an adult.)

In our example, you'll end up paying over $150,000 in interest on your $135,000 mortgage over 30 years. Ouch! But there is a way to avoid paying so much interest (besides fleeing to Ecuador).

PREPAYING

If you can afford it, consider prepaying some of your mortgage (also read our topic on **INTEREST**).

If you pay an extra $100 each month on your payment, that $100 immediately reduces your principal amount. This money not only adds to your equity, but it also makes your future payments more significant.

Why? Since your principal is smaller, your future interest payments are smaller. Your total payment due stays the same each month, but more of your future payments will go toward lowering your principal rather than paying all that interest.

If you prepay every month, your 30-year mortgage will be a lot shorter than 30 years.

STUDENT LOANS

OVERVIEW

George Orwell once wrote, "All student loans are equal, but some student loans are more equal than others." Or something like that.

Rates on student loans vary quite a bit based on the type of loan (Perkins, Stafford, Plus, etc.), school enrollment status, and when your loan started. Since policy makers in Washington like to be complicated, we can't include the giant matrix of current student loan rates. If you saw the grid, you'd hate us for even trying.

But here are some other nuggets.

TERMS

CAP is the highest amount of interest you'll ever pay on your loan.

GRACE PERIOD describes the amount of time you have, after you graduate, before you have to start repaying your loan. In some cases, interest still accumulates during this time.

CONSOLIDATING means combining all of your student loans into one monthly payment and potentially lowering your interest rate (if rates are lower now than when you originally borrowed the money). Contact your servicer for details about consolidating. You can consolidate only once. If rates go lower, you can't consolidate again.

PERKS

STUDENT LOAN INTEREST DEDUCTION

You can get a tax break on the interest you pay on your student loans, but Uncle Sam takes this perk away from you once you start to earn a bigger paycheck.

DIRECT DEPOSIT

If you set up your loan account to have payments automatically withdrawn from your checking account each month, some servicers will give you 0.25% break on your loan. Servicers feel a little security in having money automatically withdrawn for payments, so they cut you some slack. In this way, servicers are more beneficial than your tailor, who will only cut you some slacks.

SUBSIDIZED LOANS

These loans are the best. In the **INTEREST** topic, we talked about the **RULE OF MONEY**:

When you use someone else's money, you have to pay for it.

In this case, you get to break the rule. "Subsidized" means that the government pays your interest while you're in school. You get to use someone else's

money (your servicer's) without paying interest. But only for a while.

REPAYMENT

Most servicers give you a number of choices for paying off your loan. Here are the most frequent repayment options.

STANDARD REPAYMENT. Payment amounts are the same each month.

GRADUATED REPAYMENT. Payments start small and gradually increase.

INCOME-SENSITIVE REPAYMENT. Payments are a percentage of your monthly income.

EXTENDED REPAYMENT. Payments extend over 25 years (if you are eligible).

TAXES

OVERVIEW

For most people, taxes top the list of "Things I Didn't Know Anything About When I Graduated." They also top other lists, like "Reasons to Stare at My Phone and Not Make Eye Contact When Someone Starts Talking About This."

While in college, most people give their tax forms to their parents' accountant and pay a few bucks, and everything is magically completed.

Your conversation with a tax accountant is usually similar to your conversation with a car mechanic.

"Your left forward axle and suspension gaskets need fixing. That's going to cost you."

"Right. That's exactly what I thought it was."

Many people have no idea what is happening, so they are happy to shell out money each year to make the problem go away.

Alternatively, if you learn the very least that you need to know about taxes, you'll become a little bit smarter about the process.

You may still elect to have someone else do the job at the end of the year, but at least you'll have a better idea of what's happening to your money. You may save a few receipts that will earn you some tax savings at the end of the year.

Plus, now you can talk about taxes at a party and everyone will say, "Deductions? Whoa, tell me more!"

TAX EXPECTATIONS

Learning the very least you need to know means that you won't be learning everything. This book would be a lot thicker (and use far bigger words) if taxes were explained in full.

We're not going to go into every miserable detail, because, well, the details are miserable. If you wanted to be miserable, you could turn on any old Keanu Reeves movie. Plus, many tax laws are very specific to individual cases.

With that said, if you have any specific or more complicated tax questions, you should refer to a tax accountant or a tax site.

But if you'd like to get a great foundation on taxes that won't put you to sleep, this section will set you on the right path.

If any part of this chapter starts to bore you, please refer to the last page of this book.

UNCLE SAM

Uncle Sam will make a few appearances in this book, so he deserves a proper introduction. For those of you who don't know, this is Uncle Sam (a stand-in for the US government):

Originally, he was depicted extending his pinky, as in "I want YOU to make a pinky swear that you'll be the bestest friend I ever had," but the government decided to go with something more mature, like the "pull my finger" gesture.

YOUR PAYCHECK

When you first start working, you'll (hopefully) get a paycheck. If not, you may want to negotiate a little harder.

For many people, their first payday is a shocker. They hadn't expected to give away 30% of their money to things like Social Security and Medicare.

SAMPLE EMPLOYEE DIRECT DEPOSIT PAY STATEMENT

Pay Period: 04/26/2021-05/02/2021	Pay Date: 05/07/2021	Check Number: 053	Employee Number: 183	Dept Number: 1001

TAX INFO

Taxes	Total Earnings	Federal Tax	Social Security	Medicare	State Tax	City Tax	City Waiver	Total Deductions This Period
This Period:	**1081.64**	**104.11**	**67.06**	**15.02**	**40.45**	**26.53**		**253.17**
								Net Pay
Year to Date:	**20933.38**	**2868.52**	**1297.87**	**291.68**	**795.33**	**520.80**		**828.47**

FEDERAL TAX

Many factors needed to calculate

SOCIAL SECURITY

6.2% (you pay this only on roughly your first $100,000 of salary)

STATE TAX

Varies from 0% to 13.3%

CITY TAX

Only if you're really lucky

WHO HAS TO FILE TAXES?

Now that you know what comes out of your paycheck, you should also know that getting a paycheck pretty much means you have to file taxes.

In addition to federal (or national) taxes, the state, and sometimes even the city, likes to get its cut, too. No one wants to miss out on the party.

What happens if you don't file? Sooner or later, you'll get caught. As the saying goes, "Don't mess with taxes." Or is it Wyoming?

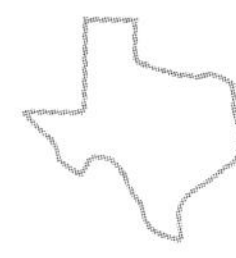

No, we're pretty sure it's taxes. If you get a paycheck, you probably need to file taxes, so don't mess around.

The problem with not filing (besides the illegality) is that you're never off the hook for the money you owe. Once you file, the statute of limitations for the Internal Revenue Service (the IRS) to audit you is generally three years.

Additionally, if you ever want to buy a home, you'll likely need to get a mortgage. Your bank will need to look at your past tax records to determine how much money you've been earning.

When you show up at the bank with an empty box, they'll probably notice that something's wrong. Then you'll have to answer to the IRS (when the bank turns you in), possibly pay fines, go to prison, blah, blah, blah.

TWO PILES OF MONEY

When you're hired, your employer is going to give you a starting salary. Let's assume that's $30,000 a year. At the end of the year when you settle the score with Uncle Sam, the government won't tax you on $30,000. Instead, they may tax you only on $22,000.

Why is that? This is the most important idea in this tax chapter:

THE MONEY YOU MAKE IS DIFFERENT FROM THE MONEY THEY TAX.

Two important piles of money exist: one pile called **Money You Make** and the other called **Money They Tax**.

TWO PILES OF MONEY

MONEY YOU MAKE
(GROSS INCOME)

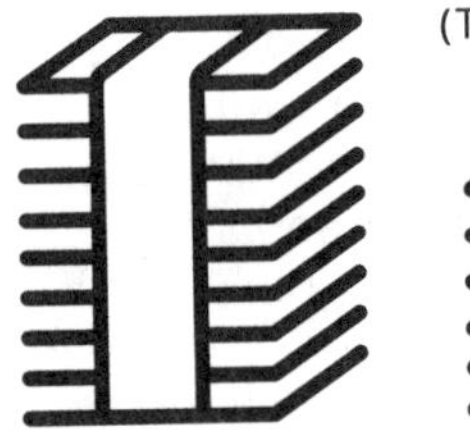

MONEY THEY TAX
(TAXABLE INCOME)

The whole exercise of filing taxes involves making your "Money They Tax" pile as small as (legally) possible.

That's why your parents spend afternoons in April (when taxes are due for the previous year) looking for receipts in the garbage. They're trying to find ways to make their income look really small to Uncle Sam so they can save money on taxes.

WHY TWO PILES?

Why is there a difference between your salary and the Money They Tax? Why don't they just give you a salary, tax it, and call it a day?

For two reasons:

BRIBERY

Everyone knows the best way to influence a ref in a big game. Everyone knows how to get a good table in a restaurant. Some people call it "bribery," but Uncle Sam calls it "a tax break." Yes, the US government plays the same games we do.

Uncle Sam bribes you to be a good citizen. He sets up random standards for "good citizenship," like buying a home, going to school, or supporting a charity. Do the right things, and he'll slip you some extra dough (fair enough).

COMPASSION

Believe it or not, Uncle Sam wants to help you. He'll give you a tax break if you have some giant financial burden, some huge medical expense, or some kids.

The government decided, "Hey, if we give people tax breaks, maybe they won't hate us so much for making them pay in the first place."

We couldn't agree more.

SASSY WORDS

As I'm sure you can imagine, a lot of time and research went into putting this book together. We spent hours reading tax books and talking to accountants, just so we could best explain the tax system to you.

In our conversations with accountants, we asked them,

"WHAT ASPECT OF FILING TAXES REALLY GETS YOU EXCITED?"

Time and time again, accountants told us that they get all hot and bothered when they hear the words *deductions* and *retirement account*. They're smoking!

Again, these are the exciting words:

- **deductions**
- **retirement account**

They might not sound attractive to you now, but they'll be on fire when you're filing taxes. They are the sassy words of accounting that make your income look smaller to Uncle Sam.

Remember how we mentioned that the goal of filing taxes is to turn the first pile (Money You Make) into a really small second pile (Money They Tax)? These are the words that will get you there. They're going to save you money.

SASSY WORD #1: DEDUCTIONS

The word *deductions* describes all the tax breaks that Uncle Sam gives away.

Remember how we said that Uncle Sam helps us in tough times and bribes us to be good citizens?

Instead of sitting down with each of us and listening to our stories like a shopping mall Santa, he gives us the benefit of the doubt. He assumes that we've all run into some tough times and done some good things over the course of the year.

So, he gives everyone an unconditional tax break of roughly $12,000 (this amount may vary some). Man, is this guy great!

You don't have to do anything, and you get a bunch of bucks off the "Money You Make" pile.

This is called the standard deduction.

Why roughly $12,000? Who knows. It's the government.

SASSY WORDS

Once you get old and mature, you'll collect more good deeds in the eyes of Uncle Sam. At that point, you'll be able itemize (or list) your tough times and good deeds.

If the total of your list is greater than your standard deduction, then you can subtract *this* amount from your pile.

What does Uncle Sam deem worthy to put on your list? The list is so random and huge that you'd need to buy a 300-page book to see all of the possibilities.

Some of the biggest "items" that you can put on your list to get above the standard deduction are:

- **gifts to charity**
- **mortgage interest**
- **state and local taxes**

If you don't own your own home or make a six-figure salary, it probably won't make sense to itemize, because your list will be too small.

Most people coming out of school just take the standard deduction.

Once you start making more money or have a huge medical expense, you may want to consult with an accountant in order to ensure that you make your list as long as possible.

Otherwise, if you're like most people coming out of school, just take your standard deduction and run. You're a good person. You deserve it.

QUICK REVIEW

Let's review. You have two piles, the Money You Make and the Money They Tax. Your mission, should you choose to accept it, is to make the second pile as small as possible using your "sassy words."

So far, you've dropped the pile with your standard deduction. Now you have one more sassy word to go.

SASSY WORDS

SASSY WORD #2: RETIREMENT ACCOUNT

It's not often that you hear people singing the praises of Sammy's tax system, but get ready: we're warming up our vocal chords.

One great thing about Uncle Sam's system is that he built an express lane for retirement savings.

He allows us to earmark a certain amount of our money for retirement in a "special box" called a 401(k), a 403(b), or an IRA (individual retirement account).

These aren't investments themselves. They're more like special boxes where you can put your investments. Within these boxes, your investments get all sorts of special powers. Most important:

Your money grows tax-free until you're old and gray.

What's so great about that? When your money grows tax-free, your account grows much more quickly than any normal account can. You are earning more interest on your interest (compound interest).

Think of your retirement account as the LeBron James of investments. It's faster and stronger than any other type of investment, because you're not taxed on it every year.

HOW RETIREMENT ACCOUNTS WORK

Most retirement accounts work the same way. You choose your investment (usually a mutual fund) and put it in your "special box."

When you file your taxes in April, you tell Uncle Sam about your box, and he'll return the money that he "wrongfully" taxed you.

For example, let's look at $2,000 of your salary. Suppose that you got only $1,400 of that amount in your paycheck due to taxes.

Instead, what if set up your special box called an IRA and invest $2,000 in your choice of mutual funds?

Since your $2,000 in salary earnings went into a retirement account (which is not taxed now), Uncle Sam will give you back the $600 that he originally took from your paycheck. What a guy!

Normal investments get taxed every year. Retirement accounts just sit nice and pretty in their special boxes and keep growing and growing with compound interest.

When you withdraw your money, you'll finally get taxed on it. (Sooner or later, Sammy will get his money.) But at this point, your money has already outpaced a comparable investment in a regular, boring taxed account.

SPECIAL RULES

These are called "retirement accounts" because normally:

You can't get to your money until you're 59½.

You'll be able to use the money for early bird specials and a new TV to watch *NCIS* on. You'll be charged a penalty if you take it out early (with rare exceptions).

You can contribute only a certain dollar amount per year to an IRA.

But the more money you make, the less Uncle Sam allows you to contribute to an IRA. Why? Uncle Sam was in a bad mood on the day he wrote that tax law.

SPECIAL RULES

A company-sponsored plan, like a 401(k), allows you to contribute more of your salary each year.

These are just a few of the rules attached to retirement accounts. Once again, nothing is simple when it comes to taxes. But these things are the least you need to know.

GETTING ONE

If you want to get an IRA, you simply go online (or visit a bank).

1. Pick virtually any online broker or mutual fund.
2. Click on "Open an IRA account." It's getting tricky.
3. Select a mutual fund (or stocks) to invest in. These are now in your "special box."
4. Yell loudly, "Hey, Uncle Sam! Na-na-na-na-na-na, you can't touch me!"
5. Sign your application and *voilà*, you're done. It's that simple.

SPECIAL DEDUCTIONS

There's one tax deduction ideal for college graduates: the **STUDENT LOAN INTEREST DEDUCTION**.

If you have any student loans, you can get a tax break at the end of the year from Uncle Sam.

This benefit starts to disappear once your paycheck gets huge. See IRS Publication 970 for more information.

TAX BRACKETS EXPLAINED

Once you've reduced your "Money They Tax" pile as much as possible, you'll need to identify the tax bracket you fall into.

Tax brackets are Uncle Sam's way of taking his cut. He believes that the more money you make, the more he can tax.

Fortunately, Uncle Sam doesn't tax all of your money at a particular rate. Rather, he taxes only slivers of money at particular "bracketed" rates. Huh?

Take a look at the example below. Try to imagine that the "Money They Tax" pile is $22,000 for you.

"MONEY THEY TAX" PILE

Of your $22,000...

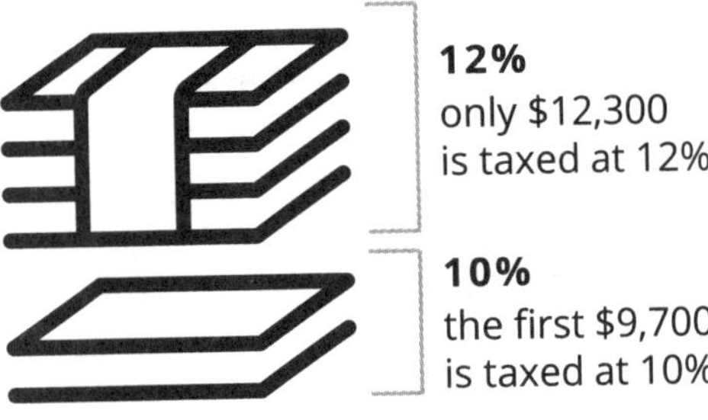

12%
only $12,300 is taxed at 12%

10%
the first $9,700 is taxed at 10%

FILING YOUR TAXES

PAY A TAX ACCOUNTANT

If you have a fairly plain-vanilla tax life, you may pay $100–$200, but prices go way up once your financial life gets more complex. You can go to a big chain or any of a gazillion tax accountants.

GO ONLINE

You'll find lots of online tax-filing options. Fill in some numbers and you're done. You'll pay less than using a tax accountant.

DO THEM YOURSELF

Filing yourself is the only (practically) free method. If you don't have a very complicated tax life, you'll be surprised at how simple this is. Visit irs.gov for forms and mail them in.

ACKNOWLEDGMENTS

THE GRADUATE'S ALMANAC

by the
Cap & Compass Writing Team

Jesse Vickey
Author, Founder

Andy Ferguson, Nicole Vickey, and Anna Pierattini
Contributing Authors

Mark Harris
Comic Artist

Alexandra Spiegel
Designer

The writing team at Cap & Compass extends thanks to everyone involved in making this book a finished product. This book is a collection of many people's experiences with life after school. The embarrassing and often funny stories told to us by friends, siblings, and seminar attendees have all made their way into these chapters. We greatly thank all those involved in the book, especially:

Macy McKeegan, Maggie Bertish, Jason Butler, Bryan Knust, and Simeon Wallis
Contributors

Denise Tanyol, Jennifer Thomas-Hollenbeck, and Laura Henry
Editors

We are also greatly indebted to the many students, recent graduates, parents, faculty members, work colleagues, tax accountants, insurance reps, apartment brokers, restaurant staff, investment advisors, and human resources managers who gave us advice, especially:

Elle Belle, Jeff, Mark, Kate, Tom, Jane, Rob, Anne, Paul, Mary, Carolyn, Jerry, Sarah, Rob (another one), Megan, Angie, the Yalies who got a free pizza, Vinny, Janice, Val, Wu, Fruitz, Melinda, Kim, Alma, Dean Sue (cute picture), Jennifer N., Steve Blond, Ashley, Michael W., and anyone we're forgetting.

MEDICINE FOR BOREDOM

If any particular page in this book bores you, please refer to the following jokes to lift your spirits.

A HAM SANDWICH WALKS INTO A BAR. THE BARTENDER SAYS, "SORRY, WE DON'T SERVE FOOD HERE."

THE BARTENDER SAYS, "WE DON'T SERVE TIME TRAVELERS HERE."

A GIRAFFE WALKS INTO A BAR. THE BARTENDER ASKS, "WHAT'S WITH THE LONG FACE?"

A TIME TRAVELER WALKS INTO A BAR.